Every Dream

INTERPRETED

Every Dream

INTERPRETED

Veronica Tonay PhD

To Neffie, and to Les, who is more.

First published in Great Britain in 2003 by
Collins & Brown Limited
64 Brewery Road
London N7 9NT

A member of **Chrysalis** Books plc

9 8 7 6 5 4 3 2 1

British Library Cataloguing-in-Publication Data:
A catalogue record for this book is available
from the British Library.

ISBN: 1-84340-051-0

Designed by Caroline Grimshaw
Edited by Claire Wedderburn-Maxwell
Indexed by Isobel Mclean
Project managed by Jane Ellis
Proofread by Michele Turney

Colour reproduction by Classic Scan, Singapore
Printed by Poligrafico Dehoniano, Italy

Contents

Introduction

We all create dream worlds every night. Often, we will surprise ourselves with the things that we do there. But what do our dreams mean? Do they help us to solve our problems? Can dreams help you to know and understand yourself better? This book will answer your questions and help you unlock your own dream secrets.

Every Dream Interpreted is unique among dream books, as it combines a dictionary of elements often found in dreams with your most frequently asked questions about them. This allows you to open and close the book at will, taking a quick glance in the morning, or having an in-depth read at bedtime. You can also feel confident about the validity of the information because it is based on research on dreams and dreamers from around the world.

The first part of the book answers the most common questions you may have about your dreams. In *Why are my Dreams Important?* you can learn the many advantages to writing down and working with your dreams. *The Dreams You Remember* outlines what everyday people dream about, all over the world. It also gives tips for sleeping well and for remembering your dreams better. *Dream Characters* helps you discover the meaning of different people and animals who appear in your dreams, including those who change into others. *Unusual and Paranormal Dreams* answers questions you may have about such topics as dreams of the dead, dream telepathy, and lucid dreaming.

The second part of the book describes the most common dream elements and presents the cross-cultural, historical, and psychological meanings of these symbols.

Anthropologists and mythologists from around the globe have made it their life's work to study symbols appearing in the art, literature, and dreams of the world's cultures. These comprise the second half of *Every Dream Interpreted*. Common dream elements and images are organized into four chapters: *The Natural Environment, Human Characters, The Animal Kingdom, and Buildings and Other Structures*. In each, you will find detailed descriptions of the many possible meanings of the people and objects in your own dreams, depending upon the specific context in which they appear.

Every Dream Interpreted provides you with a plethora of information about the many possible meanings of your dreams. But remember that no book can interpret your dreams for you; you created them, and only you can unlock their meaning.

Who will benefit?

This book will appeal most to people who are interested in dreams and dreaming: curious, intuitive, creative, sometimes introspective, open-minded people. Psychotherapists and pastoral counsellors will find this book helpful to use with their clients, as it aids inner exploration. Those interested in literature, art, or film; those who want to use their dreams for personal or spiritual growth; teachers; and those leading dream workshops and dream groups will also find this book beneficial and easy to use. But perhaps this book will most aid those in relationships that matter to them. By sharing dreams with loved ones, we also share ourselves. Developing a dream sharing group—even a community of two—enhances intimacy and understanding in a meaningful and refreshingly playful way.

How to use this book

Before beginning to explore this book, buy or create a dream journal for yourself. It helps to have a special book in which you can write your dreams. Some people prefer to write both dreams and daily reflections and thoughts in the same journal, so that they can see the relationship between their dreams and their daily life. Others feel more comfortable keeping their dream lives separate from their waking life. In either case, having a book and a pen by your bed at night does help to increase the number of dreams you remember.

Once you've found a journal, you may then want to flip through Part One, reading the questions and answers that appeal to your curiosity. If you have trouble remembering your dreams, read the tips on dream recall. If you have trouble sleeping, it may comfort you to know that in a study done in 1991, 36 percent of adults in the U.S. had some kind of insomnia. Almost everyone has a hard time sleeping when coping with life's challenges, and it is difficult to remember dreams when your sleep is poor. Help for a good night's sleep can be found in the first chapter.

Practice the sleep and dreaming tips until you have a few dreams to work with, or ask if you can borrow some dreams from a friend. Then map out a general interpretation of those parts of each dream addressed in the question and answer section. That may feel like enough for now, and you may want to stay at that level of interpretation until you feel quite comfortable with it.

Once you're ready to move more deeply into your dream world, venture into Part Two of the book, the Dream Directory, which elaborates upon the information found in Part One, giving more detail about individual dream images. You might take with you a particularly puzzling, vivid, unusual, or memorable dream, since these dreams often contain more symbols than dreams about real-life people and events. Try underlining each of the elements in the dream for which there is an entry in the Dream Directory. Then make notes on the meanings outlined for each element, placing a star or other symbol by those that immediately strike and stay with you. Finally, rewrite the dream, inserting the *meanings* you've discovered in place of the original dream images.

If you encounter an image that doesn't yield itself to interpretation, let it rest for a while. Dream incubation (see page 60) can often illuminate those stubborn dream elements after a few nights.

Recording your Dreams

A single dream will probably not tell you very much about yourself. Rather, it is the dream themes that revisit us over time that illuminate hidden places inside us. Keep track of your dreams over a week, a month, or longer. Some studies found that it takes between 50 and 75 dreams to get a true sense of one's dream themes. Making your dream world a priority, and doing so again and again throughout your life, is a way of exploring your own history. Your dreams will then become the chronicle of your life.

What are the most widespread and accepted ideas among dream experts about why we dream? For thousands of years, philosophers have speculated on exactly what our dreams mean about us. They arrived at many different conclusions, some of them contradictory. It wasn't until the 20th century, though, that psychologists started trying to figure out which of these ideas about dreaming were correct. In this chapter, you'll find the four main dream theories used today by dream experts. How did we discover which of these holds the true key to dream interpretation? Well, we're still searching, but we have some answers. Read on…

The history of dream research

Discovering dreams

Most of what we know about dreams and dreaming we have learned in the last century. What do dreams say about our waking lives? In order to answer that question we need to explore them in depth.

Freud

Modern dream research began around 1900, when the Viennese physician Sigmund Freud published the first psychological book on the topic, *The Interpretation of Dreams*. His research on dreamers was based on clinical case studies and he wrote about the dreams of his patients in what would later be called psychotherapy. He also wrote about his own dreams, using self-analysis to try to figure out what his dreams meant, as many of us do each morning. Freud initially concluded that dreams express those unconscious wishes, usually either sexual or aggressive, that we cannot admit to our conscious minds because they would cause us too much distress or would disrupt our sleep. Later, Freud added that dreams may express unresolved emotional trauma, and he also developed a system of symbolic interpretation for dreams (see page 78).

Freud's initial goal in using dream analysis was to help his patients become aware of unconscious feelings and thoughts that were mainly being manifested in physical symptoms. He wanted primarily to help his patients become free of enduring inner constraints imposed upon them in early childhood. He also found that dreamwork helped him to understand the unconscious relationship patterns his patients would enact with him.

Jung

Many other early psychologists shared Freud's interest in dreams, most notably the Swiss physician, Carl Jung. Jung, who worked primarily with schizophrenics, studied his own dreams and those of his patients in an attempt to test and expand upon Freud's theories about dreaming. To that end, Jung travelled around the globe, collecting dreams from people in a variety of cultures, some of them relatively untouched by the Western world. He noted similar, recurring themes in images that appeared in the dreams and visions of people far removed from one another, and also in the hallucinations, dreams, and art of schizophrenics.

From these observations, Jung developed his theory of the collective unconscious and its *archetypes*, patterns for human experiences that we all share and which are expressed in our dreams. He differentiated between "big," or *numinous*, archetypal dreams, in which these universal patterns appear, and "little," or *personal unconscious* dreams, which express our own personal concerns and history, and can be interpreted using Freud's theory. Jung was most interested in numinous dreams, which he defined as being rare, especially vivid and memorable, with a mythological quality. Numinous dreams also contain archetypes, which can be interpreted. (See box opposite for descriptions of the four main archetypes and how they may appear in dreams.)

>

Numinous vs. Personal Unconscious

NUMINOUS	PERSONAL UNCONSCIOUS
Archetypal, "big" dreams	"little" dreams
Vivid and memorable (they can stay with you for years)	Less vivid and memorable
Mythological (similar in structure and theme to a folk tale or fairy story)	These are related to the everyday concerns of life
Contain archetypes	Contain "real life" scenarios and characters

CONTINUED >

Numinous Dreams

Numinous dreams may appear at the important junctures of your life. These dreams can reveal previously unknown feelings and thoughts about the situation in which you find yourself. When you have these kinds of dream, you might also consider whether some previously unknown quality within you is just below the surface, pushing to become conscious through the dream. (Archetypes are also discussed further on pages 208–211.)

One or more of these four main archetypes can be found in many numinous dreams.

Persona

The *persona* is the social role(s) we play in the world and even to ourselves. It is who we think we are, and who we would like others to believe we are. In dreams, it is represented by such things as masks, objects, clothing (and nakedness), and settings associated with work. When these appear in a numinous dream, ask yourself if there is some way in which you are confusing yourself with your social role.

Shadow

The shadow is who we think we are not, and contains both positive and negative qualities. Shadow qualities are close to consciousness and usually can be seen by people we know well. The shadow appears in dreams as a creature, animal, or person who initially threatens and/or chases us, but as we become aware of its qualities, our dreams may change so that we start to act in unfamiliar ways. Consider whether the shadow figure that seems to want to harm you may actually have a different agenda. Perhaps it wants to contact you and get to know you. It is, after all, just your unknown face.

Anima/animus

The *anima* and *animus* represent our psychological femininity and masculinity, respectively. In order to call a quality masculine, it needs to be something manifested by *most* men, across cultures, and across time. The same is true for feminine qualities. The dream *anima* in her positive aspect is usually a female figure, receptive to others, emotional, and seeking harmony, whereas the *animus* is a male who is active, logical, gets things done, and is discriminating. In her negative, exaggerated aspect, the *anima* may appear witch-like or hysterical, and the *animus* may be almost demonic and without feeling. If you dream of these figures, ask yourself whether they might represent some quality you need in your life. If they offer guidance, or lead you somewhere, pay close attention to the information they impart as Jung believed they could lead us to our souls.

Self

The *self* contains the entire psyche, all that we are and are not aware of about ourselves. The self is represented in dreams as a *mandala*—a symmetrical figure, often a circle. Other self-images include the tree, with its roots deeply implanted in the ground and its branches reaching upward. *Mandalas* in dreams are very meaningful as they indicate that you are on the right path, or (if the *mandala* is fragmented or incomplete) how far you may yet be from your true self.

Jung also felt that all dreams are *compensatory* to waking awareness: what you dream about yourself is previously unknown to you, and the dream informs you in an effort to balance your psyche. In other words, if you dream that you are very angry with your spouse, you are probably not aware of just how irate with him you really are. The anger is disrupting not only your relationship in the outside world, but your inner emotional and physical states. This disruption appears in exaggerated form in the dream. In this example, the shadow appears in the dream as the raging dreamer. Such a dream is certain to get your attention. If you then ask yourself, "Am I really angry at my husband?" you will be well on the way to discovering something important you weren't aware of before.

The goal of Jungian dream interpretation is to help the dreamer to express as much of the true, whole self as possible.

Gestalt

In the 1960s, a group of *Gestalt* psychotherapists concluded that contrary to Freud and Jung's views, the unconscious was unimportant to understanding dreams, and instead declared that all parts of your dream *are you*, as you are in the present. Gestaltists observed in their work with patients that dreams represented issues and concerns that were left unfinished in the dreamers' waking lives. In order to help dreamers overcome these issues, Gestalt dream therapists prefer to work with groups, having dreamers act out each character and object that appear in their dreams. You become the chair, the road, your husband etc., and >

as you do so, you learn what kinds of things various parts of yourself are feeling and believing.

Gestalt therapists found that people hide from parts of themselves in order to avoid pain, and dreamwork helps them to rediscover these "split-off" parts and become whole again. For example, if you dreamed of a beaten dog walking up a steep road, while acting the part of the beaten dog you might say, "I am so tired. I just want to get home. I've been beaten and I'm hurt and exhausted." As the road, you might say, "I am narrow and constrained and hard." From such a dream, you might learn that part of yourself makes things harder for yourself than need be, that you "beat yourself up" by being overcritical of yourself, that this inner battle exhausts you, and that you should maybe practice being softer.

Phenomenology

The last main dream theory is *phenomenology*, originally described by Medard Boss. Boss writes that dreams should not be interpreted at all, but rather should be taken as they are, as another mode of being. The goal of dreamwork is to help dreamers see themselves as they really are, as they experience themselves in their dreams. A person who dreams of machines and metal, for example, is encouraged to

The Four Major Dream Theories

Freud: dreams represent unconscious sexual and aggressive wishes and fears that originated in childhood and are disguised in dream symbols.

Jung: focus is on numinous dreams of the collective unconscious, which represent the psyche's striving for wholeness; archetypes are interpreted.

Gestalt: all elements in a dream express parts of the dreamer; dreams illuminate disowned or fragmented aspects of the self and are explored by being acted out in a group.

Phenomenology: dreams are simply another state of awareness and express our way of being in the world; avoids all forms of interpretation.

recognize that their way of being in the world is mechanistic and lacking in feeling.

Which one is correct?

Each of these four main dream theories, although very different from one another, is still used in psychotherapy to help psychologists interpret their clients' dreams. They are also used to form questions for those dream researchers interested in studying what dreams really mean about a person.

In order to find out if any or all of these theories are correct, we need to gather a lot of dreams from many different kinds of people and find some systematic way of studying them. One attempt to do that was launched in the laboratory in the 1960s. Sleep researchers hooked participants up to an EEG that measured their brainwaves during sleep. From this research, scientists learned about the four stages of sleep; REM (dreaming) sleep; and NREM sleep (see page 28). Later, they found that when they woke up sleepers during REM sleep, the sleepers would remember their dreams.

At around the same time, psychologists (being more interested in what dreams meant about the person having them than they were in the biology of >

sleep) were collecting thousands of dreams in an effort to determine what the majority of people dream about. The leaders of that effort were psychologists Calvin Hall and Robert Van de Castle. Hall and Van de Castle used a random sample of dreams they collected from 500 men and 500 women and subjected it to an extremely detailed coding system. They coded each dream using categories such as aggression in the dream, friendliness, sexuality, misfortune, good fortune, emotions, characters, and setting. Because they developed such a specific way of coding each dream, their study could be replicated by others, and hundreds of studies using this coding system have been published. (To code your own dreams, see the box "Are Your Dreams More Like a Man's or a Woman's?" on pages 88–89.)

How do researchers study dreams now?

Those who study dreams these days tend to use some type of coding system, or one of the four main theories about dreaming as a starting point. Researchers either investigate a long dream series from one person, or the dreams of many members of a certain group (e.g., liberals, obsessive people, pregnant women, artists etc.), or a set of a certain kind of dream (most recent dreams, dreams of being naked, dreams of marriage etc.). Some studies on dreaming don't use dreams at all! Instead, researchers distribute surveys asking people whether they have ever had a dream of falling, for example, and then asking them other questions about themselves (e.g., "do you feel you are afraid of success?") in an effort to determine the meaning of falling dreams. Surveys tell us less about dreams than do the other methods of studying them. Because surveys rely upon people's estimation of what they dream about and how often, surveys often lead to other kinds of studies where dreams are collected and coded in some way.

How many dreams are needed?

Each kind of study yields different results. Studies of specific kinds of dream or on certain groups of people that reach conclusions based on fewer than 50 dreams, are probably not reliable. Most agree that it takes at least 25 dreams from the same person to say much about that person. One hundred dreams is much better, because once you've reached 100 dreams, slight variations from dream to dream become eclipsed by the sheer amount of dreams. So the more dreams you have, the more you can learn about your own dream world. (For tips on remembering more dreams, see pages 71–74.)   >

Ways Dreams are Studied

In the laboratory, using EEG and other equipment to relate dream content to physiological processes.

By collecting sets or series of dreams and using one or more of the four main dream theories to interpret them.

By coding dream series or sets on various categories, and then relating these to waking personality or behavior.

Distributing surveys which ask dreamers about different aspects of their dreams.

One Dream Interpreted From Four Perspectives

Several years ago, I was interviewed on National Public Radio regarding dream interpretation. I was given a dream from a female listener and asked to very briefly interpret it from each of the four perspectives discussed above.

The dream: you graduate from college, get your degree, begin your life, then you get a phone call and learn you're missing three credits. The missing credits are in either mathematics or gym, so you haven't legitimately graduated.

Here are four very general interpretations, meant to help you see the differences between the major perspectives. Of course, in-depth interpretations are beyond the scope of this book.

Freud

Dreams represent unconscious aggressive or sexual wishes and fears. Freud might say that there is, perhaps, a masochistic wish in the dreamer to fail and to return to childhood, so this might be a dream about the fear of success. Institutions often represent the mother, so the dreamer may be expressing how she unconsciously feels about her parents thwarting her as a child. She may also have internalized her parents who won't let her "graduate," or grow up.

Jung

Dreams represent universal human experiences and parts of ourselves we are coming to know. If this were a numinous dream, it would represent the collective experience we have with institutions. College is a very masculine (active, logic-based) institution, and so are gym and mathematics. This dreamer may feel unsure about being able to express her masculine side in the world and may need to learn to do so at this point in her life.

Gestalt

All parts of the dream represent the dreamer. There aren't any other people or objects in the dream, so the dreamer might act out what mathematics or gym is like for her. Perhaps she needs something in her life at the current time that doing these activities provides.

Phenomenology

Dreams represent the dreamer's way of being in the world. Therefore, the dreamer is in a state right now where she feels that something has not been completed.

Studying your own dreams

When you remember your dreams, what are you really remembering? Are you recalling the dream as it actually happened, or a distorted, partial version of the original dream? Because we cannot yet record dreams as they occur, the only person who really knows what you dream about is you. All that dreamworkers and researchers know about dreams comes from dreams written down or told to us. We don't know if we have accounts of real dreams as they took place, or of elaborated or even made-up dreams. But because many of the answers to the questions here are based upon research performed on tens of thousands of individual dreams and dreamers from all over the world, the information is more likely to be accurate than it would be if I were just giving you my personal opinion. After all, anyone can say that dreaming of water means that you're going to win the lottery or find a lost object, or that you are a flowing person, and so on. But does it? To find out, we rely on researchers.

After the publication of my first book, The Creative Dreamer, *I've fielded questions on dreams from hundreds of callers to radio programs. As a university teacher and psychotherapist, I am asked daily some question or another about dreams. Most of these are reproduced in Part One (and the answers, too!). Feel free to browse this section and experiment with some of the exercises. Have fun!*

Questions and Answers

Why are my Dreams Important?

IT CAN TAKE SOME effort to remember and write down your dreams. Why go to the trouble? Here, you'll find all the ways people find their dreams helpful, as well as some general information about sleep and dreaming, and tips for getting started interpreting your own dreams.

What is a dream? What is a nightmare?

Dreams

There are so many definitions of dreams and
dreaming. But most of us who actually work with
dreams agree that a *dream* is the metaphorical
picture story that results from thinking while asleep.

Nightmares

A *nightmare* is just a fearful dream, one that produces
anxiety in the dreamer. What scares you in your
dreams may not scare you in waking life, and
vice versa, which is why you must feel afraid in
order for a dream to be called a nightmare.

We know *mare*, in nightmare, as a word
meaning a female horse. Horses, as you will learn in
the second part of this book, are thought by some
to symbolize sexuality, especially the emerging
sexuality of young women. In fact, the word "mare"
was originally derived from an Old English myth
about an evil spirit (an *incubus*) that lies on top of
people and tries to destroy them by suffocating
them while they are asleep. Mythology held that
an *incubus* also attempted to have sex with sleeping
women. Another interpretation is derived from
Sanskrit, where "mare" means "the destroyer."

If we put all of these meanings together, "nightmare" might translate as: something that happens in the night, involving women, an evil spirit, and sexuality. Interestingly, far more nightmares are reported by women, and most involve being chased or attacked (but rarely killed) by a hostile male figure of some kind. (See Part Two for more on nightmares.)

How and when do we dream?

In a typical night with eight hours of sleep, you will dream several times. Although some people swear they never dream, sleep laboratory studies show that everyone has, on average, five dreams per night. Most dreams are quickly forgotten, however, and the majority of us remember only one to two dreams per week.

Stages of sleep

Each night, we cycle through two kinds of sleep: REM sleep (with its fast, active brainwaves and rapid eye movements) and NREM sleep (slow-wave, quiet sleep). As we fall asleep, we move from an alpha (or waking) brainwave pattern to stage one sleep. If you watch someone just falling asleep, you will notice their eyes begin to make slow, rolling movements. They will quickly pass through stages two and three, and after about half an hour will reach stage four. In stage four, brainwaves actually look, on an EEG, like those seen in people who are in a coma. The cerebral cortex (the part of the brain responsible for higher mental functions) slows down, and blood pressure, breathing, and heart rate decrease.

After about another half an hour, the dreamer returns to stage one, and now has their first dream. At this point, you may notice that their eyes move more quickly and more sharply than they could if the person were awake. (Although it seems the dreamer must be actually tracking the dream action with their eyes, studies trying to link rapid eye movements with dream memories have been inconclusive.) These eye movements show that the person has entered the first REM period of the night, and the brainwaves now resemble those of a person who is awake and experiencing panic. No matter what they are dreaming about, their breathing, heart rate, and blood pressure become irregular, and both men and women show sexual arousal. At this stage we are unable to regulate body temperature so we often shiver or perspire.

Dreaming sleep

From this first REM period, the dreamer descends again to stages two, three, and four, rising again to another REM period (stage one), but then alternates between stages one and two for the rest of the night. The REM sleep stage (stage one) repeats about every 90 minutes. REM sleep is called *dreaming sleep* because most dreams occur during REM, and people who are awakened during this stage often remember what they were just dreaming about.

It is also possible to dream in other stages of sleep, and sleep >

researchers have observed that people can dream immediately after falling asleep—before REM—and also during NREM. *Night terrors*, particularly intense and terrifying dreams, typically occur in NREM.

Dreams and REM

However, the majority of dreams are likely to occur during the REM stage of sleep. The longer you sleep, the longer REM lasts (up to 40 minutes)—and the longer your dream lasts, the more likely you are to remember it, especially from later in the night.

One study found that dreams in a single night tend to be variations on a theme. It seems that dreams from earlier in the night are based on current situations. Mid-sleep, dreams incorporate memories from long ago. Before we wake up, we dream again of more current life situations.

Some experts believe we use our dreams to seek solutions to current problems by searching through our memories for previous situations in which we faced a similar conundrum, re-examining our memories, and then using previous ways of

coping to deal with the current situation. The dream then becomes a way of experimenting with various, previous solutions to a problem.

Other experts hold that "time traveling" in our dreams from early to late in our sleep cycle suggests that dreams and memory are linked, with dreams perhaps serving some important, more purely biological memory function.

The purpose of dreaming

Despite over one hundred years of research, no one knows exactly why we dream. Because we all do it, and because it is an important part of sleeping (with sleep culminating in more dreaming the longer one stays unconscious), scientists agree that dreaming is important. Whether dreams help us to learn by transferring information from short-term to long-term memory, or keep us flexible in our thinking by activating various groups of brain cells, or serve to balance our emotions or express our secret desires, dreams do relate to our lives in predictable and fascinating ways. And whatever purpose dreams serve, REM sleep is necessary for life. But don't worry if you are afraid you are not getting enough sleep to survive, as it takes a month or two of REM sleep deprivation to kill an animal. That much REM deprivation is not possible in humans because, when we are deprived of REM sleep, we automatically experience the REM *rebound effect*, which means we have more REM the next time we sleep. This explains why people who stop using drugs that suppress REM sleep will temporarily recall many more dreams).

Stages of Sleep

Falling asleep: eyes make slow, rolling movements.

Stages 2 and 3: quickly passed through.

Stage 4: brainwaves resemble comatose person. Cerebral cortex slows, blood pressure decreases.

Stage 1: first REM period (1 hour after falling asleep). Eyes move more quickly and sharply, brainwaves resemble panicked awake person, physiological indicators become irregular, dreamer is sexually aroused.

Dreamers cycle through stages 2, 3, and 4, returning again to 1/REM sleep and alternating between it and stage 2 every 90 minutes for the rest of the night. REM periods lengthen throughout the night.

How are dreams different from daydreams?

In order to investigate daydreams, researchers asked people to carry pagers with them throughout the day, and randomly paged the participants, who had to note down exactly what they were thinking at the moment the pager went off. The researchers then coded the responses using a variety of categories.

These researchers found that daydreams are much more fun than dreams! They tend to be pleasant and end happily, with the daydreamer starring as the hero. Our daytime musings are often used as rehearsals for real-life action, being more focused and goal-directed than are our dreams. Try recording your own daydreams (see the box on page 35 for a sample) and compare them to your dreams.

Daydream differences

As with dreaming (see page 84), men and women daydream differently. Male daydreamers report that they daydream most often of competition, success, and sex, while females mainly daydream about friendly interactions with others.

Typical dreams, on the other hand, are usually unpleasant. Dreams and daydreams both address our current concerns, but daydreams seem to show us what we would *like* to be true, whereas dreams show us what we *believe* is true.

Dream Notepad

28 March

10 am: daydream I completed the project (somehow!), gave it to Madeleine (my boss), and she loved it. Not effusively, but I could tell she thought it was brilliant. Felt great! Now, if only I can get started.

3 pm: daydream Julia takes the project over. Relief!

29 March

Dream: I dreamed I met with Madeleine. I didn't finish the project. She stood up and started screaming at me. I felt 9 years old.

2 April

Dream: I am summoned by a sort of queen. She is dressed in red and she asks me something. All the time, she is distracted. I get annoyed. I'm ready to do her bidding, but she won't pay attention to me. I feel like a loser.

*O*ften in my dreams I am running away from something or someone and I feel like I have lead feet. I can't run quickly, and sometimes I can't even move! What does this mean?

One of the most fascinating facts about dreaming is the answer to this question. The human body has developed to protect us from all kinds of situations—even from the possible dangers of our own dreaming mind.

*D*ream paralysis

During REM sleep, our major muscle groups are deeply relaxed. Our vital organs naturally still function (including the heart muscle), but our legs, arms, hands, feet, and neck are nearly completely paralyzed. At the same time, our brains are creating lots of stimulation from within, but our legs and arms don't "know" that the dreaming brain is creating the stimulation. If our limbs were not so deeply relaxed, they would respond the way they do to the brain's response to incoming stimulation from the "real" world: if someone is chasing you, you start running! Fortunately, being paralyzed during REM sleep keeps you from getting up, acting out your dreams, and possibly hurting yourself in the process. However, if a person is damaged in the area of the brain responsible for REM paralysis, they will begin to physically act out their dreams while asleep.

While your brain bombards your limbs with signals as if what you were dreaming were really happening to you in the outside world, it also recognizes that your legs, feet, arms, hands, and neck are not responding to the signals reaching them and that you are not moving. So, how does your brain make sense of this? It creates a dream.

Dreams influenced by REM paralysis

A variety of common dreams expresses the paradox of moving but not moving. The dream of falling mimics the feeling of not being able to move to save oneself while moving through space. If you dream of being pursued and unable to move quickly enough, remember that you are having the most common human dream: being chased!

Moving in slow motion and dreaming of being paralyzed mirror what the body is actually experiencing during the dream: seeing, feeling, and experiencing, but being unable to move. Because there are sound physiological reasons for these kinds of dream, it is probably wise not to lend them too much psychological meaning.

What do flying dreams mean?

One researcher, Anthony Shafton, uses flying dreams as an example to illustrate the many interpretations a single kind of dream can have. He asked a number of different experts about the meaning of flying dreams and was given a total of 24 different answers. Although some of the interpretations seem to just be variations of one another, he concluded that each dream can have many different meanings, and all of them may be correct. The emotional state of the dreamer; the time the dream occurs; what is occurring in the dreamer's life; the dreamer's background, experiences, personality, and culture—all of these may influence the dream and its meaning.

Psychological interpretations

What do psychologists say about flying dreams? Freud saw in flying dreams a symbol for sexual potency (in men) or for surrendering to sexual temptation (in women). Alfred Adler, an early psychoanalyst who broke away from Freud and developed his own theories, wrote that ambitious people tend to have flying dreams, reassuring us that

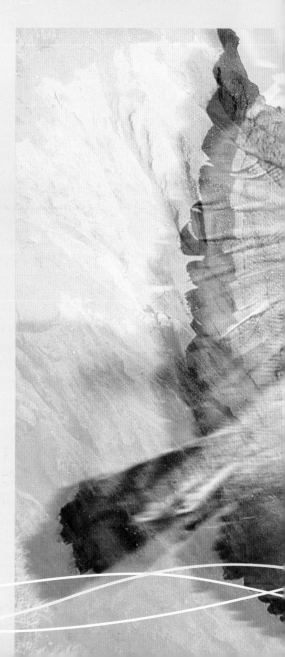

surmounting what would be impossible in waking life is actually easy. Others see flying dreams as evidence that one has gone beyond oneself, is too "high up" (see pages 174–177) and ungrounded in the real world, or is seeking to escape from responsibilities in waking life.

Linguistic interpretations

Flying and the direction "up" are naturally associated. In English, words that represent movement in that direction are positive: when exuberant, we are "flying high"; we "climb" the stairway to success; we feel "free as a bird." Freedom, happiness, and carefree abandon are also associated with flying in dreams. If you dream of flying, are you feeling this way in waking life?

Dreams of flying may also represent your feelings about achievement. Do you view yourself as a successful person, flying high? Are you happy and content soaring about? Or are you concerned about failure (that you might fall at any moment)? Are you flying at all, or is it too difficult to "get off the ground"?

Whatever your own flying dreams may mean to you, enjoy them. They are among the most memorable and invigorating of all dreams. Some practitioners of lucid dreaming are even able to make themselves fly in dreams using dream control (see pages 174–177).

What do dreams mean about a person, if they mean anything at all?

Experts argue both sides of this question. Some sleep scientists and biologists believe that dreams are nothing but brain chatter, random neurons firing at will. Dream researchers retort that dreams are related to people's personalities, life experiences, and waking life preoccupations—they are individual and personal. Those who work with their own dreams or the dreams of others note how uncanny it can be to recognize something important within oneself or another person through a dream.

Dreams and waking behavior

Accounts of dreams from therapists working with clients and findings from studies demonstrate that dreams do relate to waking behavior and personality. Dreams are neither random nor bizarre; they represent the brain making sense of the world, mostly conveyed through images. Since the majority of us depend upon verbal language to communicate thoughts and ideas, the image and feeling-based language of dreams can be puzzling, but the second part of this book will help you to understand it.

Dreams and feelings

Dream research demonstrates that we behave and think in dreams in a similar fashion to the way we do in waking life. If you are a friendly person, you will have lots of people in your dreams, and many positive interactions with them. If you are a hostile person, then aggression will be the predominant factor in your dreams. The characters in your dreams will mirror your beliefs and attitudes about people when you are awake, and the settings and familiarity of the landscape and people who populate your dreamscape reflect back to you how foreign or welcome you may feel in the world just now.

(See "Your Dream Personality," on page 43.)

Although we behave similarly in dreams and waking life, our feelings seem to be very different. You can see this most clearly in dreams in which you are in a situation that would normally elicit terror (e.g., being chased by a tiger), but in the dream you are calm and laughing. Perhaps by presenting us with feelings we don't (or can't) acknowledge or consciously experience while awake, dreams help us to balance our emotions. For example, mildly depressed people tend to have more happiness in their dreams, whereas happy people tend to   >

have more sadness. The difference between our feelings while we are awake and our emotions in our dreams is most pronounced in the dreams of trauma survivors.

*D*reams and trauma

In early October 1989, I began collecting dreams at the University of California at Santa Cruz, the town where I live. On October 17th, the Loma Prieta earthquake struck just a few miles from the campus. Most students at UCSC are from California and are used to earthquakes, but this one was larger than any in my lifetime. It brought down a section of the Bay Bridge in San Francisco, nearly 100 miles north, and completely destroyed most of the beloved downtown area of Santa Cruz.

Intuitively, I expected the worry and fear of the students to spill over into their dreams, but I was wrong. In fact, no one remembered any dreams at all for the first few nights after the earthquake, despite repeated disruption of REM sleep due to dozens of scary aftershocks in the middle of the night. The first dreams students remembered were almost childlike: happy, playful scenes in which dreamers seemed to be returning to an earlier way of coping with their fears. One week after the earthquake, other characters in the students' dreams started to become anxious and frightened, while the dreamer observed them dispassionately, with no clear indication about what had caused the unpleasant feelings in those around them. Two to three weeks after the earthquake, most dreamers had incorporated aspects of the quake itself into their dreams, and began to report feeling afraid in their dreams.

Other researchers, including those studying the Oakland firestorm, the Southern California earthquakes, and Vietnam War veterans, found similar results. Some dream experts have observed a similar pattern in their work with psychotherapy patients who suffer trauma. These studies show that dreams may help trauma victims make sense of what happened and integrate their experience into the rest of their lives.

Your Dream Personality

You will need several dreams for this exercise—the more the better. Think of yourself as a character in a film or novel. Your series of dreams is the script or book, and you (as you are in the dreams) are the protagonist. What kind of person is this character? How would you describe them? Look through your dreams, underlining any phrase that describes the protagonist (i.e., describes you). Now, circle any of the words or phrases below that describe you as you are in your dreams (these descriptors were found to best describe the widest variety of people's personality characteristics), or add others:

- outgoing
- introspective
- warm
- keep to myself
- focused
- easygoing
- observant
- oblivious
- stable
- a bit wild
- creative
- practical

Next go a bit further and consider how the protagonist sees other people and the world. How do they expect others to behave? What do they think of their work? Do they seem more comfortable in natural surroundings or in the city? Will they easily trust others, or are they more guarded? How do they typically spend their time?

Asking and answering these questions may give you some new insights into your own personality. If you're feeling brave, swap dreams with a friend and see yourself and your dreams through their eyes.

Can you diagnose physical illness from dreams?

Some people have dreamed of a serious physical condition before being diagnosed. Anthony Shafton describes dreams of "plugged pipes" in a person with blocked bowels, a patient who dreamed of a dry riverbed and was diagnosed with circulation problems, women dreaming of refrigerators and other cold places before learning their fetuses had died, and many other fascinating cases where people seemed to know they were ill.

Inner signals

These instances are uncommon, though. What may well be happening in such cases is that while we dream, our bodies are sending our brains barely perceptible, subliminal signals which are then translated into the visual metaphor of dreams. Outside sensory stimulation is reduced during

dreaming, so it may be easier for our brains to pay attention to these inner signals as we sleep.

Most often, though, when people dream of a physical problem, the condition is either a metaphor for something with which they are currently struggling, an actual known past or present condition, or an illness the dreamer fears.

Consider the following terrifying dream, dreamed by a woman with no history of womb problems, and no diagnosis of such:

"I dreamed I was being eaten from the inside by some kind of creature. It was in my uterus, eating its way out. It was horrifying. I don't remember feeling any pain, just knowing it had to get out, it would get out, there was no way to hurry it."

This troubling dream illustrates one problem with dreams that may look as though they signal an illness. This dreamer had no history of problems with her womb, she did not have any children, and wasn't pregnant. Very physically active and healthy, she was so concerned about the dream she arranged an appointment with her physician, who assured her after examination and tests, that her uterus was perfectly healthy. However, this woman had suffered chronic sexual abuse as a child, and was at an intense and important juncture in her psychotherapy.

Why do other people's dreams often seem so boring?

I always laugh when I hear this question. I don't find other people's dreams boring at all! The reason I don't has to do with my experience exploring their meaning. As a clinical psychologist, I work with my clients' dreams every day. I know these people intimately and listen to their dreams carefully, seeking insights into their unconscious motivations and feelings. Gathering years of experience with over 20,000 dreams and hundreds of dreamers also means that I listen to what someone is dreaming about in a different way to someone who has no idea about what such dreams might mean.

Once you have read this book, other people's dreams may suddenly seem fascinating to you. Your friends and family may freely tell you about their dreams, from which you can (if you choose) guess all kinds of things about them. You might even get a glimpse of the way in which they perceive you. It might be best to keep your insights to yourself, though, as people rarely like to have their secrets revealed.

$\mathcal{A}$ boring dream?

Imagine, for example, your friend tells you the following dream:

"I am swimming alone in the sea. Suddenly, out of nowhere, a huge wave appears. It is like a tidal wave. I am terrified I will drown and I wake up."

This is a relatively common dream, especially for those who live near the sea. On the surface, it seems banal. But suppose, after reading this book, you've learned that water is the one element that dream experts agree upon: it represents the unconscious (especially feelings of which we are unaware), the substance from which new life arises. Your friend seems to be having some emotional difficulty just now. It leaves her feeling quite overwhelmed and anxious, questioning her ability to cope. She is alone in the dream, suggesting she may also be feeling isolated. Now that you have some insight about how she might be feeling, you can choose to give her what she needs. Suddenly her dream no longer seems as dull, does it?

Why should I go to the trouble of writing down my dreams and working with them?

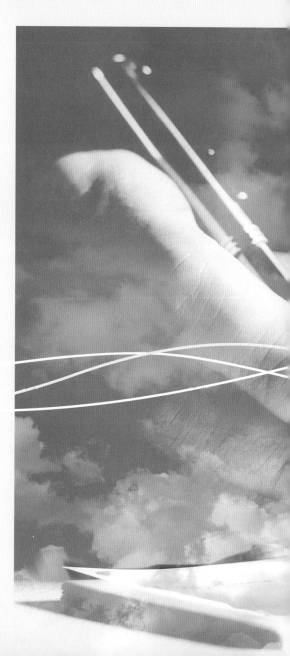

Dreams tell you the truth about who you are. You are the author of each of your dreams, and you can only create from what is already within you. The more you know about yourself, the better you will be able to negotiate the world. If you know yourself, you are more likely to know others, and if you know others, you can not only choose friends who are appropriate for you, but you can be a better friend to people you know well. You will also probably be more effective in all of your worldly efforts, since you'll be more likely to place yourself in situations, and surround yourself with people that suit you, and vice versa.

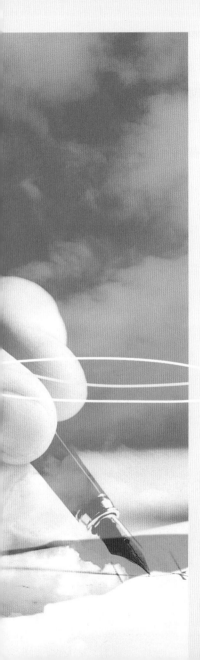

Dreams as mirrors

Although most of us would like to hide from ourselves at times, persistent dream themes can show you "blind spots" about your negative and positive qualities. Just as most of us are unaware of at least some of our less charming traits, many of us don't realize we have our own hidden talents—those unique and even wonderful aspects of ourselves. Dreams show you how you behave, how you most typically attempt to solve problems, and the quality of your relationships, because they are pictures of how you think of others, society, and the world. They demonstrate your beliefs about the way in which others are likely to treat you, the conflicts you may be feeling, where you might be stuck in life, and even suggest ways to move forward. They are also one way in which we are all creative.

If you're reading this book, you are probably already interested in getting to know and understand yourself better. Being able to care for others in a kind and conscious way is likely to be important to you, and understanding and befriending your dreams will help you with these goals.

What can I learn about myself and others from exploring my dreams?

You can learn a bit about other people when exploring your own dreams. However, your dreams mostly show you the ways in which you *view* other people, how you feel about them, and what you really believe.

Revealing interactions

Take a look at all of the dreams you have had about different individuals in your life. Are there themes that reoccur? Are you always joyful and playful with your girlfriend, but feel tense and uncomfortable around your brother? Do you find yourself arguing with a particular friend and running from people you don't know? These themes deserve closer examination. They would indicate that, when awake, you may be unaware of some conflicts with your brother and your friend that are distressing to you, perhaps deeply, and are showing up in your dreams. You may feel unsafe or threatened by strangers, and most comfortable with your girlfriend.

Looking at the patterns of your interactions with everyone in your life as they appear in your dreams should give you an indication of the quality of your feelings for them, the enduring satisfactions

and the challenges you face. Once you start to consider how you are feeling in those relationships, you can initiate conversations, choose to behave differently, watch your thoughts about them, consider how you are contributing (or not) to harmony between you, and so on. Or. you can just marvel at the complexity of your own inner life.

Distressing dreams: what to do

For example, callers on radio shows on which I've been a guest will often ask something like, "I keep dreaming my husband is having an affair. Should I be worried? I am so mad at him in the morning!" I give several responses to these kinds of calls. >

First, you should never, ever accuse a person of something as serious as betraying love vows on the basis of a dream, no matter how natural it may feel to do so. Being angry with someone else after waking up from such a dream is natural, but acting on that anger is unfair. Give yourself some breathing room, relax, and consider.

Dreams are not oracles or psychics—they are reflections of your own mind's thoughts and feelings. In reality, all you know for sure is that this dream reflects something going on inside of you. You made this dream up yourself. Why would you torture yourself by giving yourself such a disturbing dream? Do you disturb yourself with such thoughts when you are awake?

Second, perhaps (just perhaps) you are picking up on something about your husband that has left you feeling insecure. This may or may not mean an actual affair is taking place, but it would reflect your feeling that your husband is not attending to you in the way you might like. If that rings true, also consider whether or not your own behavior toward your spouse has changed. Where is your heart? It could be time to have a close, loving, "tune-up" conversation about how each of you is feeling.

Third, you may not be dreaming about a third person at all! It may be that the dream is demonstrating to you that your husband is having "an affair" (or would like to) with some aspect of your own self. What is the "other woman" like? Is she the sultry, sensual woman you haven't had time for lately? Or the on-the-edge, self-confident lady? Have some fun. Act out that part of yourself with your husband, or even in front of the mirror, alone. See what happens!

Understanding others

In addition to showing you how you feel, think, and behave around other people, dreams also reflect your preferred activities, locales, and your feelings and thoughts about these. It's fun to gather a number of dreams of close friends or loved ones and notice what they are actually doing in their dreams. You can learn quite a lot about how others (and yourself) spend their time just by looking at what they do in their dreams. Sharing dreams with another person or a group of friends will tell you things about them that you might never have observed or realized in the waking world.

New solutions

Finally, dreams can help illustrate new solutions to old problems, and to provide creative inspiration.

Is it really possible to get creative inspiration or to solve problems by attending to my dreams?

When a client has been "stuck," unable to see his or her way out of a longstanding problem or pattern, often that problem will appear in a series of dreams. (See "Chasing a Dream Theme," on pages 62–63 to identify such a pattern in your dreams.) If you already know what the problem is, you might try dream incubation to help solve it (see page 60).

Science and art

There are lots of accounts of scientists, artists, and writers who have used their dreams for inspiration. One of the most well-known of the scientific discovery stories involves Friedrich August Kekulé von Stradonitz, the famous chemist. He saw a metaphorical image in one of his dreams that helped him to discover the molecular structure of benzene. The image was of a circular snake biting its tail, and this led the chemist to consider that benzene might be structured in a ring.

Dozens of artists, predominantly the Surrealist painters, used dreams as inspiration for their work. Dali, Magritte, Rousseau, Matisse, and many others titled their works after dreams, or wrote about their use of dreams in creating their art. Although their work might be considered strange, creative people's dreams are no more bizarre than anyone else's.

Famous Writers and Dreams

It would be hard to imagine the genre of fiction if it did not include dreams as one of its literary devices. Several prominent novelists and poets, including Stephen King, Walt Whitman, Edgar Allen Poe, Graham Greene, Henry James, T. S. Eliot, W. H. Auden and D. H. Lawrence, have used their dreams as inspiration, to dissolve creative blocks or to resolve thematic questions. Author, John Fowles, in his classic work of psychological literature, *The Magus*, seems to almost create one complex, rich dream through his writing.

Creative people

When studying creative people's dreams, I found that, in general, they tend to be more interested in dreams, and therefore remember more of them, as well as recalling them more vividly, than the general population did. Their dreams are populated with more children, fear, and themes of loss than are the dreams of less creative people. This may be because creative people often suffer difficult childhoods, which they are able to transform into productive, artistic work later in life.

Dreams and coping

How likely are you to be a person who is able to cope with life's problems? The answer might be in your dreams. Studies show that, for women, the more dreams you have in which you are independent and self-reliant, the more likely you are to be able to cope well with feelings arising from life crises, and to successfully resolve problems related to life transitions such as divorce.

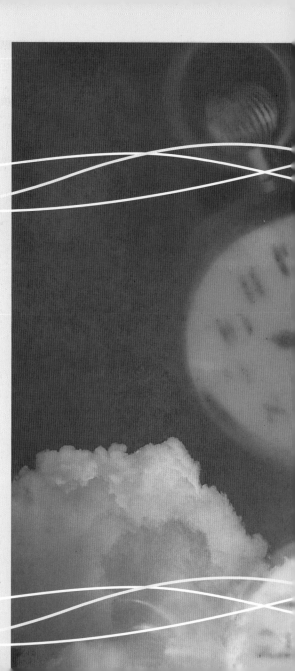

Is it true that dreams have influenced the course of history?

Dreams have always played an important role in hunting and gathering societies, when members would have great dreams that would influence the entire group. Over time, dreams have been important in many cultures during times of societal crisis (war, famine, etc.); as an important basis for belief in the soul; for the creation of myths; for coping with illness; and during life transitions.

Ancient uses of dreams

Dreams were given a special place in society as far back as two millennia ago, when the first book on dreams, *The Oneirocritica*, was written. Some ancient cultures, such as the Egyptians and Mesopotamians, felt the gods communicated to humans through dreams. Dreams were used to solve problems, heal illnesses, and even to decide if, when, and where to wage battle.

The ancient Greeks identified a god of sleep (Hypnos) and a god of dreams (Morpheus) and believed that gods entered through keyholes in doors and spoke to dreamers while standing nearby. They believed even their most powerful god, Zeus, spoke through dreams to tell mortals their fates. >

CONTINUED >

However, in the second century BC, Aristotle, the Greek philosopher, began to think psychologically. He wrote, as did Sigmund Freud two thousand years later, that those most adept at interpreting dreams must be able to see resemblances between things occurring in the outer world and the dreamer's culture and own past experiences. Only by looking at all three realms could one accurately interpret a dream.

Dreams and religion

Old Testament and Talmudic Hebrew stories illustrate that prophets were given divine guidance through dreams. The famous story of Moses being told that God would speak to him in a dream illustrates how important dreams were considered to be as ways to experience God. A number of Christian saints later wrote about the importance of dreams in coming to know God, including Saint Augustine in the fourth century. A thousand years later, however, the Church considered dreams (especially erotic dreams) to be sinful and tempting—the work of Satan. If one analyzed one's dreams for meaning, one was seen to be doing the business of the Church, since it was felt at that time only the Church could interpret the word of God. Dream interpreters were therefore committing heresy! After the Dark Ages passed, philosophers began once again to examine dreams and dreaming, and as they started to link dreams with personality, observing that dreams reflect one's character, Christianity again accepted dreams as worthy of further study.

Non-Christian cultures have also looked to dreams. In medieval times, Chinese officials used dreams for problem solving, and Japanese dream interpreters used dreams for healing. Muhammad discussed his disciples' dreams with them, and accounts of famous Muslim dream interpreters date from the first century AD. In 1000 AD, thousands of Muslim dream interpreters practiced their skill, and seven hundred years later the first Muslim dream dictionary was published. Muslims did not consider dreams to be diagnostic of medical conditions as did the Greeks, but they did base some military actions on dreams, and linked dreams to prophetic statements in the Koran.

There are a number of stories about inventions and artistic creations that were inspired by dreams (see page 54). But can we accurately say that dreams have changed history? Certainly not! People change history. The dream we have may not be the dream we remember, and the dream we remember may not be the one we write down, tell, or act upon in the morning.

The Importance of Dreams in History

Dreams played an important role in many cultures. Some ways dreams were used at various times in human history include:

• As messages from the gods.

• To heal illness.

• As prophetic oracles, helping societies decide where to hunt, when to wage war, when to move, and so on.

• To create myths.

• To solve problems.

$\mathcal{T}$here is a pattern in my dreams, a story which leaves off and picks up again, night after night. How can I delve more deeply into this dream theme?

In my first book, *The Creative Dreamer*, I wrote about several common dream themes (children, loss, nature, and being blocked by others) that appear in the dreams of people who consider themselves (and are likely to be) creative people.

$\mathcal{I}$dentifying dream themes

When you are struggling through a difficult or challenging situation or transition in your life, you may notice this phenomena: your dreams leave off at one point in a story and pick it up again, perhaps the next night, perhaps a few weeks later. For example, you may have several dreams of being around or in a farmhouse, trying to get to a path on the other side. Weeks later, you dream you are walking down a path and turn around to see a

farmhouse behind you. Or, you are being chased, as one of my clients was recently, by a prehistoric beast at the seaside. Some days later, you dream you are at a dinosaur theme park, riding a beast that looks uncannily like the one in the first dream.

Such themes can develop over time, as well. If you've written down your dreams over years—even just a few—you might have inadvertently been recording an evolving dream theme. Over the next few weeks, watch your dreams for recurring elements or storylines. (See Part Two of this book to help you identify them and see "Chasing a Dream Theme," on pages 62–63.)

Chasing a Dream Theme

Part One

Give each of your dreams a title, for example, "the monster emerges from the ocean," or "the men keep coming after me." Then, consider each of your dreams as if you were back in primary school, writing a simple book report, where each dream is a book. Your goal is to summarize the dream in two or three lines. For example, imagine you've had the following dream:

"I am back in the house I lived in as a child, but it is somehow different. The rooms are larger, with more light. There is no one there, and as I explore, I start to feel panic. There are many more rooms than in the original house, and I keep going forward."

You could call this dream "exploring my childhood," or "hidden rooms in the past," or even something literal and simple like "childhood house." You might summarize it in this way: "I'm in my past, which has changed. I'm afraid, but keep going." For part two of this exercise, note the feelings you wrote down that occurred within the dream (in this case, panic) and then ignore them for the moment.

Once you have a number of dreams to work with (25 is about the right amount), number each dream from 1 to 25 (or however many dreams you have), then sort through your titles and summaries, grouping those dreams that have elements in common. (If you want to, you can write each dream onto an index card, which makes sorting easier.)

Now, put the largest stacks of cards into numerical order and read through them. Do you see a story evolving? Is there a way in which this story relates to something you're concerned with in your daily life? Examine your dreams over the next few days after doing this exercise, and check for any progression of the theme. Often, your dreams will "answer" your questions for you.

Part Two

Now group your dreams by the emotions you felt in them. Put all those containing anger (including frustration, irritation, rage, etc.), apprehension (worry, anxiety, dread, etc.), fear, sadness, and happiness in five separate piles (if using index cards), or make a five-column chart, noting the number of each dream containing each emotion (see below). Some dreams may appear in more than one column.

Dream Emotion Chart

EMOTION

Anger	Apprehension	Fear	Sadness	Happiness
1	6	2		22
4	13			
19				5
21				
24				

For this dreamer, dreams 1, 4, 19, 21, and 24 all contained anger, making anger the most common emotion expressed. There was no mention of sadness in the dream series. An abundance of—and an absence of—a specific emotion can be important in dreams. This dreamer might want to look at the ways in which she is feeling sad in everyday life, and the degree to which she is expressing it.

Examining your most common feelings in dreams can be revealing. In this case, the dreamer might ask, why am I angry in the dream? Does this mirror a feeling I am having in my waking life? Is there a way I can become more aware of feelings of anger, and perhaps express them appropriately if I need to?

Dreams with a common emotional tone tend to make up a dream theme. They can help us to balance our emotional life by making us more aware of important feelings in our waking lives, and helping us to identify and respond differently to those situations that make us vulnerable . . . or happy!

The Dreams You Remember

By COMPARING THE DREAMS of people around the world, this chapter aims to bring to you a sense of shared humanity, as you realize how similar our dream lives are. A questions and answers section will guide you through the meaning of symbols and important dream themes such as childhood and pregnancy. You'll also find tips for sleeping better, healing nightmares, and techniques for remembering your dreams more vividly.

$\mathcal{I}$ don't sleep well, and to dream, I must sleep. Please help!

All kinds of things can interfere with your ability to go to sleep, to sleep through the night without interruption, and to wake up when you'd like to. Sleep experts repeatedly warn that using alcohol and other drugs is one of the most frequent causes of insomnia and sleep disruption.

$\mathcal{A}$lcohol disrupts sleep

Alcohol slows down the central nervous system and disrupts normal sleep. Drinking at night, after your evening meal, is almost guaranteed to produce a bad night's sleep. You may feel sleepy after having a drink, but it will change your normal sleeping pattern (see pages 28–33 on sleep cycles). In the middle of the night, when the effects of alcohol subside, you are likely to wake up and then find it hard to fall back to sleep. Alcohol also relaxes the muscles in your throat and changes your breathing pattern, making snoring more likely. Sleep clinics, when testing people for sleep apnea and other sleep disorders, give patients small amounts of alcohol before sleep to determine how bad a person's breathing difficulties can get.

>

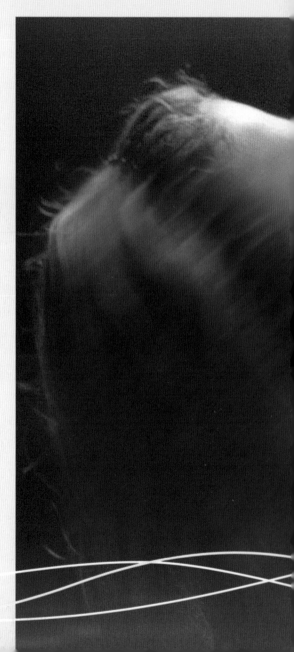

Food and sleep

As for food helping or interfering with sleep, studies show that calcium and tryptophan (found in warmed milk, among other things) promote sleep, and that caffeine disrupts it. Although many people feel that melatonin is helpful as a sleep aid, no scientific studies have shown this.

Emotional difficulties

Depression and anxiety both interfere with sleep. If you are sleeping a lot more or less than usual, wake up more frequently, or have trouble falling asleep, you should seriously consider seeking professional help from a psychotherapist, counsellor, or physician. Prolonged sleep disruption can have negative effects on your health and feelings of well-being.

Scents for sleep

Lavender and jasmine scents
have been found to promote
relaxation and sleep. Use these
essential oils in an oil burner or
in the bath: sandalwood,
cedarwood, and rose are also
good. Lavender mist sprays are
available at many health-food
stores; spritz your pillow before
bed. Or clip a few sprigs from a
lavender plant and crush them in >
your pillowcase.

CONTINUED >

Tips for Sleeping Well

• Get some exercise during the day as it not only helps you sleep better, but also staves off depression. However, don't do aerobic exercise within two hours of trying to sleep. Just before sleep, slow stretching can relax you.

• Don't eat just before you go to sleep. An early evening meal rich in carbohydrates with very little or no protein may help to relax you. Some people believe that a baked potato eaten an hour before bed is a natural sleeping pill.

• After you've eaten your evening meal, start slowing down. Avoid television just before sleep; it's stimulating to the nervous system. Try reading a good book, listening to soothing music, or talking to a good friend instead.

• Sex is a wonderful way to get better sleep!

• Just before bedtime, drink a glass of warm milk—it contains tryptophan and calcium, which are natural sedatives. Chamomile tea is also known for its relaxing effect.

• Avoid all caffeine after mid-afternoon as its effect on your body lasts many hours after ingestion! Remember that caffeine can be found in several over-the-counter cold medications, soft drinks, and chocolate, as well as in tea and coffee.

• Avoid drinking alcohol after your evening meal.

• If you're feeling stressed, try writing about your problems. Several studies have found that people who keep a journal and record their troubles tend to feel less anxious.

• Develop a ritual that you perform every night before you go to sleep. Some people make their tea or warm milk, write in their journal, pray or meditate, and then read for a while. Making these practices a regular part of your life helps your mind prepare for sleep.

• Take a warm bath for about 15 minutes. Staying in longer might lower your blood pressure too much, and a hot bath will actually stimulate your body and make it harder to sleep.

• When you're in bed, take a deep breath through your nose and hold it in. Close your eyes, relaxing the muscles of your face, and lightly press your fingertips together. Hold them that way for about five seconds, then slowly exhale through your mouth. Relax your hands and repeat several times until you feel relaxed.

• Locate and release any remaining tension spots in your body by taking several deep breaths, imagining yourself sinking into the bed. Then, beginning with your toes and slowly progressing up your body to your shoulders, tense, hold briefly, and release each part of your body. When you reach your neck, lift it up off the bed and hold it for a few seconds, then let it fall back. Squeeze your eyes shut and release them, too.

• Visualizing yourself performing a calming activity can help you shed problems your mind seems preoccupied with. Imagine yourself rowing across a wide expanse of water (you probably won't make it to the other side before you fall asleep!), stretching out on a sparkling beach, or hiking in lush wilderness. This can relax your body and leave you feeling calm.

• If you wake up frequently during the night, you might try wearing soft earplugs. Some people are very sensitive to noise when asleep. Alternatively, waking up often can signal the need to reduce anxiety in your life.

I never remember my dreams. What can I do?

Simply reading this book should boost your dream memories, since motivated people typically remember more dreams than those uninterested in dreams.

*M*ore tips to help you remember

Keep a pen and paper by your bed each night. Buy, or even better, create a dream journal that is used only for that purpose. Let your unconscious know you are serious about remembering your dreams. Just before falling asleep, write the next day's date on an empty page of your dream journal.

Before you go to bed, have your spouse, partner, or a friend (or even you, yourself) tell you that you will remember your dreams tonight. You can even remind yourself several times during the day if remembering your dreams is particularly difficult. Writing yourself dream reminder notes and hiding them in places you will come across helps, too.

Share your dreams regularly with another person. Dream sharing is a lovely way to become closer to those you care about, and it also increases dream remembering.

Get lots of sleep, because the longer you sleep, the more REM periods you have, and the more dreams you will have to remember. Taking naps after you've had a full night's sleep also works well.

If none of the above helps you to remember more dreams, set your alarm for a random time each night for a week . . . instant dream recall!

Have someone sleep with you and wake you up when they notice your rapid eye movements. (Just don't hit them when they do.)

If you usually remember your dreams, but are suddenly unable to, think back to what you did with the last dream you remember. When a dream has been misinterpreted or ignored, dream recall often slows down or stops.

When I wake up it's as if my dreams start to vaporize. It's so difficult to catch hold of them. Are there techniques I can use to remember them while I examine them?

Some people have an easier time remembering their dreams than do others. My own study demonstrated that the main thing that recalling lots of dreams means about you is that you are motivated to remember them, and are interested in them.

Personality and dream recall

A number of people have examined whether people who remember their dreams are more introspective, introverted, or mentally unstable; or more stable, happy, or intelligent. Although creative people do remember slightly more dreams than less creative people, and genuine clinical depression does result in less dream recall (antidepressants and many other medications, alcohol, and most illegal drugs suppress dream memories), no other personality trait has been associated with remembering (or not remembering) your dreams.

Thus, the good news is that if you want to remember your dreams, are reading this book, and put paper and pen by your bed at night, it's likely you will begin to remember your dreams. The more you want to remember them, the more you will remember.

How to record your dreams

You need a quiet environment in which to write them down or tape record them immediately upon awakening. As soon as you wake up in the morning, keep your eyes closed and go over the dream in your mind in as much detail as possible. Be determined not to fall back asleep. After you open your eyes, immediately write the dream down. Don't wait! We have only about three seconds after opening our eyes to remember our dreams without

rehearsing them in our minds first. This is because the outer world with its sensory bombardment disrupts dreaming sleep, and it seems that dreams are encoded in memory in a different way to waking experiences. Speed in recording them is the key to remembering your dreams.

If you find it hard to write in the morning, or have awoke from the dream in the middle of the night, you might invest in a hand-held tape recorder or lighted pen. With a little practice, you should be able to speak or write clearly enough to understand yourself in the morning.

What kinds of dreams do most people have?

Most dreams are unpleasant! It seems that dreams focus in particular on more difficult emotions. Dream researchers found that in most of the dreams in which the dreamer experienced some kind of good fortune, they then began to worry about it, or the good fortune turned into a misfortune.

Many studies have found that if you were going to predict your next dream, you'd be most successful if you guessed that it would contain you and two other characters (90 percent of adults' dreams include two other adults, while in only 15 percent of your dreams are you alone). Your next dream is most likely to occur inside a building of some kind, but not your own home. It would also contain hostility and be generally unpleasant—in about two-thirds of most people's dreams, a misfortune strikes or anxiety is felt. This percentage is larger for sex dreams, which often end badly, reflecting performance anxiety, relationship fears, or fear of being caught.

Sexual dream experiences are somewhat rare, occurring in about 10 percent of young men's dreams and between four and eight percent of women's. These frequencies may increase toward

middle age, with, in one study, 30 percent of women's dreams containing explicit sexuality. (See pages 84–87 for differences between men's and women's dreams.)

Most Common Human Dream

This dream exemplifies the elements most commonly occurring in the dreams of human adults worldwide: I am inside the communal hut/coffee shop/neighborhood bar. My friend and a stranger are with me. The stranger begins to argue with me, then gets up. I run away toward the door to the hut, but then it falls to the ground with a loud noise. I am afraid.

How can I tell if something in my dream is a symbol? Is a cigar ever just a cigar?

Is it a Symbol?

A dream element is likely to be symbolic if it:

- appears in more than one dream
- is vivid
- evokes strong feelings within the dream

The Directory will help in understanding dream symbols that may appear in your own dreams!

Sexual symbols

Sigmund Freud (see page 12), wrote that everything convex and elongated (cigar, tower, hose) was phallic, representing the penis, whereas everything concave and indented (cave, purse, hole) represented the vagina. He noted that the feelings of guilt, shame, and desire that the genitals aroused in people in Vienna in 1900 could be too threatening to the conscious mind to be represented straightforwardly in dream imagery. The mind therefore disguised the real, underlying, latent content of the dream (the genitals and the dreamer's feelings about them) in the manifest (or storyline) content of the dream.

For example, imagine that a man dreams of driving his red sports car into a small garage, and just as he pulls in, the roof collapses, destroying

the car. A Freudian might say the dreamer is afraid that sexual intercourse will leave him damaged as a man in some way.

*P*ower symbols

Most modern psychologists find the symbolic aspect of Freud's dream theory incomplete, but it was investigated by a creative researcher who found that threats to convex and elongated objects in dreams ("castration anxiety") correlate with the amount of power women hold in various cultures: the more power women hold, the more dreams people in that culture will have in which elongated objects are threatened. In other words, phallic objects in dreams seem to be symbols of power, not of the penis. A man who dreams of his garden hose being cut in half by his boss is likely to be expressing his fear that his boss will destroy his sense of personal power, not actually castrate him.

Do people's dreams from around the world contain basically the same themes?

The dreams of people all over the world are remarkably similar. One of the things I love about studying dreams is that we are all so alike when we dream. I'm comforted to know that a hunter in Zimbabwe is most likely having a dream similar to mine.

Our dreams unite us

Although the specific elements and settings are certainly different (fancy restaurant versus savannah), the concerns we all express in our sleep identify us as part of the human community. We are all born, we grow up, mate, are generative, lose loved ones, and die. We all have similar feelings about these experiences, no matter where we live. Researchers have studied dreams from many traditional tribal societies. They found that tribal dreams were mostly similar to those of people from the United States and other industrialized societies, However, the amount of physical violence was quite different. Almost every small or tribal group studied had more violent dreams than Westerners did, even those from the U.S., whose violent dream percentage (and rate of real-life violent crime) exceeds that of any other industrialized society.

Remember that we behave in dreams as we behave in life. Tribal societies are steeped in life-sustaining activities, which include contact with the origin of their nourishment. Westerners, on the other hand, rarely witness the violence done to animals which sustains us.

Violent Dreams in Different Cultures
(violent dream percentages)

SOCIETY	MALES	FEMALES
Yir Yiront	92	n/a
Baiga	86	n/a
Navaho	77	n/a
Skolt	70	68
Ifaluk	60	40
Tinquian	55	46
Alor	53	61
United States	50	34
Hopi	40	39
French Canadians	n/a	31
Dutch	32	14
Swiss	29	23

Can you determine someone's personality type by looking at their dreams?

A few studies have tried to link waking personality with people's dreams, but the results were not as extensive as you might think, considering that so much of ourselves appears in our dreams. Some aspects of your personality do appear in your dreams, but bear in mind that most of these findings come from studies on college students. (For research on psychiatric groups, see pages 108–111.)

Type A personalities (driven people who experience almost constant inner pressure) have more disturbing dreams than Type B personalities (calmer, relaxed individuals).

People who report dreams in the "twilight" portion of sleep (dreams that occur as they are falling asleep) tend to be less anxious, more poised, self-accepting, and less conforming than people who don't remember such dreams. Those who don't recall "twilight" dreams tend to be more authoritarian in waking life and also behave in a typically authoritarian way in their dreams: they conform to the group and condemn those who don't.

Sensitizers (people who are aware of their anxiety and tend to feel it more strongly) tend to dream more often of future events and of the past than do people who repress their feelings when awake.

What do your Dreams Say about Your Personality?

IF YOU DREAM...	YOU ARE LIKELY TO BE...
• disturbing dreams	• Type A
• just as you're falling asleep	• less anxious, more poised, self-accepting, less conforming
• of the future and past	• a sensitizer
• of unusual settings, loss, children, obstacles in nature	• creative
• of everyday scenarios	• introverted
• emotional dreams	• a thinking type

Creative and less creative people also dream in different ways. Creative people place their dreams in unusual, varied settings (compared to the more frequent home dreams of less creative people); dream of creative pursuits; have dreams of loss, children, and trying to overcome obstacles in nature; and the frequency of their sexual dreams varies with whether or not they are actually doing something creative in their waking lives. Intuitive people (who tend to be creative) remember more "big," numinous, archetypal dreams (see page 13) than do people who prefer to take in information through their five senses.

Introverts (people who focus on the inner world of ideas and feelings, whose energy is directed mostly inward) recall more "little," everyday (vs. numinous, archetypal) dreams than do extraverts (those whose focus is mostly on the outer world of people and events). However, extraverts and introverts tend to recall archetypal dreams just as often. (See page 13 for a discussion of these two types of dreams.)

Thinking types who make decisions based on logical analysis tend to have more emotions in their dreams than do feeling types, who decide based on principle and values.

Are men's and women's dreams different or the same?

Even though our dreams are mostly similar no matter who we are, adult men's and women's dreams show some fascinating differences.

Universal sex differences

Research on dreams worldwide demonstrates that women dream of people they know, who are equally likely to be male or female. Interactions are equally likely to be friendly or aggressive, but most often take place indoors, in a familiar setting. Therefore, a typical woman's dream would take place inside her home or workplace, with familiar people with whom she is interacting in some way.

Men's dreams are usually set outdoors, with characters most often male and unfamiliar. Men's dreams of other men are usually aggressive. When men do dream of women, their interactions tend to be friendly. In the most common man's dream, then, the dreamer is outdoors with a hostile, unfamiliar man or group of men.

Obviously, men's and women's dream themes are quite different! Although a few studies failed to find these differences (African-American and native Japanese people's dreams may differ), thousands of

dreams from dozens of cultures demonstrate these sex differences. Researchers speculate that these dreams reflect our real-world experiences. For men, the world can be a hostile place in which they must compete with unfamiliar men—a task from which they may find relief with women. Women are most concerned with cooperative, harmonious relationships with individuals of both sexes. Also, studies show that a woman's self-esteem comes from feeling successful in her relationships, whereas a man's self-esteem arises from success in the competitive world of work.   >

Why are they different?

Most of us have heard that women are more
comfortable with their emotional life than men are.
There is actually an emotional problem called *male
alexthymia* that describes how difficult it is for many
men to express their feelings in words. Women are
raised in the world of emotion, and if self-esteem
for them comes from relationships, then being able
to express feelings is very important. But at work,
expressing feelings can actually block success.
These differences find their way into our dreams,
where women experience more feelings than
do men.

Sex differences in sex dreams

What about erotic dreams? Unlike their portrayal in
films, most sexual dreams are unpleasant. Think
about your last erotic dream. Who were you being
sexual with? If you're a man, most likely you were
dreaming about sex with someone you don't
know, possibly someone who doesn't exist in the
real world. (If your partner is a man and you are
now recoiling in horror, don't worry! In the

section on sexual dreams, we discover they are rarely about real relationships.) If you are a woman, your dream was probably about sex with your partner or a partner from your past. If you are a young woman, you might have felt nervous about being caught. Otherwise, you probably had feelings of closeness and, perhaps, uneasiness about your partner's feelings.

Cultural changes and sex differences

These differences between men's and women's dreams remained constant between the 1950s and 1990s, despite social changes, such as the sexual revolution and more women becoming better educated and entering the workplace. Several studies,

including my own in 1990, found that although women show more aggression in their dreams and more feeling than they did in the 1950s, women's dreams haven't changed substantially since then.

On pages 88–89 "Are Your Dreams More Male or Female?" allows you to see if you dream more like a man or a woman. If you are a woman and your dreams are similar to a man's, you may have an unusually well-developed masculine side. If you're a man and your dreams are like a woman's, you may be more expressive of your femininity. Remember that you cannot determine someone's sexual orientation from looking at their dreams, and these differences are about psychological maleness and femaleness, not about sexuality.   >

Are Your Dreams More Male or Female?
Part One

For 10 consecutive dreams, make a chart with three columns labeled **character**, **sex**, and **familiarity**.

• First, write down all the characters that appear in the 10 dreams in the first column (characters include each person, animal, or group ["a crowd," etc.]), but do not include yourself in the list.

• Add up the total number of these characters and divide by 10 (the total number of dreams). This will give you figure (A).

• Fill out the sex column for each character (except animals): denote male, female, or mixed sex.

• Fill out the familiarity column (for humans), putting a tick against any person(s) you know.

• Add up the total number of male and total number of female humans. Divide the total number of males by the total number of humans to give (B). Repeat for females to give (C).

• Add up the total number of familiar humans and divide by the total number of humans to give (D).

• Insert (A), (B), (C), and (D) into the chart below to compare your results with the average. On the whole, are you closer to the average number for men or for women? Do you dream more like a man or a woman?

		YOU	AVERAGE MAN	AVERAGE WOMAN
Characters/dream	(A)		2.4	2.8
Percentage Males	(B)		.53	.37
Percentage Females	(C)		.26	.40
Percentage Familiar	(D)		.45	.58

Are Your Dreams More Male or Female?
Part Two

Characters	Sex	Familiarity
Bob	male	x
My cat	--	x
A crowd	mixed	--
A woman	female	--
Marco	male	x
Male stranger	male	--
Female strangers	female	--
Winnie	female	x

A = 8/10 = .8
B = 3/7 = .43
C = 3/7 = .43
D = 4/7 = .57

This dreamer has fewer characters than is typical, suggesting a person who interacts with fewer people when awake. With an equal percentage of males and females, and more familiar characters, this dreamer dreams like a woman.

How much will my dreams change during my lifetime?

Studies of people undergoing psychotherapy suggest that in that particular situation, one's dreams can change quite a lot. However, a number of case studies of very long dream series spanning decades demonstrate that, in general, dream elements and themes and the concerns they represent do not change very much across one's adult life. (See pages 98–99 for information on children's dreams.)

Why don't they change?

The first explanation is that dreams reflect a deep part of our personality, our core traits that remain stable despite our life circumstances and the situations in which we find ourselves. These core traits show themselves in our dreams.

Another possibility is that dreams originate in or tap into long-term memory, and the events that made up those memories are in the past and are unchangeable. Dream themes and images resulting from your long-term memories would therefore repeat themselves over time, making your dream life seem quite stable across your lifetime.

The last possibility is that when you look at your dreams across your entire lifetime, the main concerns of humans in general are those that repeat

themselves. The bizarre few months of dreams you had when you were 25, or the dream series you had during Jungian analysis, may not be representative of the entire series, which seems unchanging just because of the sheer number of dreams you've recorded.

What does change?

Of course, the people in your dreams will change as the people in your life change, as will your incidental interests and dream activities. Life-cycle changes can bring temporary changes in dreaming, too. For example, increased nightmares during times of difficulty or trauma, themes peculiar to pregnancy (see page 95) and challenges you face as you age will all be represented for periods of time in your dreams.

How will my dreams change as my pregnancy progresses?

First of all, you will have more dreams. Hormonal (progesterone) changes in pregnancy increase dream recall and vividness. Regularly waking up during the night, which is common during pregnancy, also increases dream recall.

Pregnancy stages and their dream themes

A few studies on pregnancy and dreaming discovered that pregnant women tend to have particular dream themes at different stages of pregnancy. Probably these are not due to hormones or other biological influences, but rather due to changes in the woman's body, relationships, and self-image during pregnancy. For example, research on elements appearing in pregnant women's dreams compared to non-pregnant women's dreams found a greater than average rate of buildings both big and small, reflecting body image changes as expectant mothers swell. Pregnant women also dream more often than others of their own mothers; sometimes their mothers even give birth for them. Across their pregnancies, pregnant women dream more often of animals, which become increasingly large and more similar to humans as delivery approaches.

>

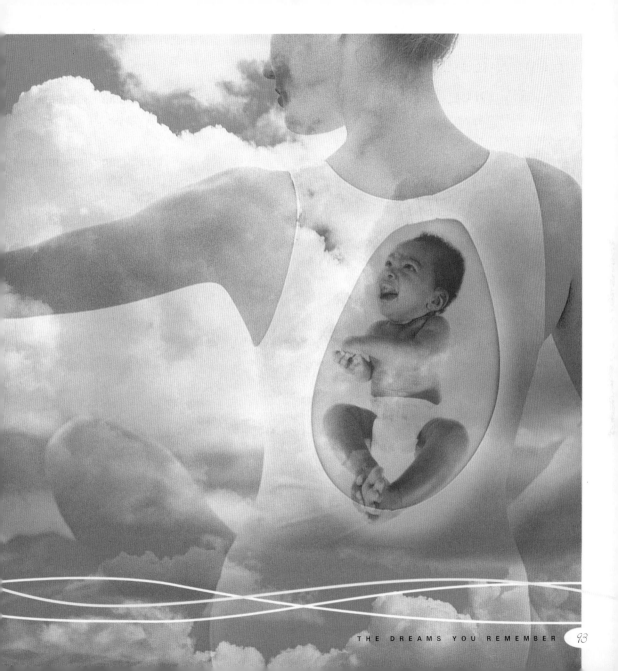

CONTINUED >

First trimester

Other dream motifs change with each stage of
pregnancy. Early on, women may feel nervous
and frightened about pregnancy and childbirth. In
this stage, women may dream of their babies
suddenly appearing, being born with little or no
labor, or being born as small, talking adults with
wide vocabularies.

Second trimester

In the middle part of pregnancy, women dream
more often of giving birth to a deformed baby or
animal. Dreams of friendly animals (which are
relatively rare in dreams at other times) may
represent the dreamer's revisitation of her own
childhood by animating the stuffed animals that
once comforted her, or may illustrate a friendly
relationship between the woman and her basic
mothering instincts (instincts are often represented
by animals in dreams—see Chapter 7).

Third trimester

These dreams are replaced by those in which the
woman is undergoing difficult labor. One study
found that the more anxious dreams a woman has
during pregnancy, the less likely she will be to have

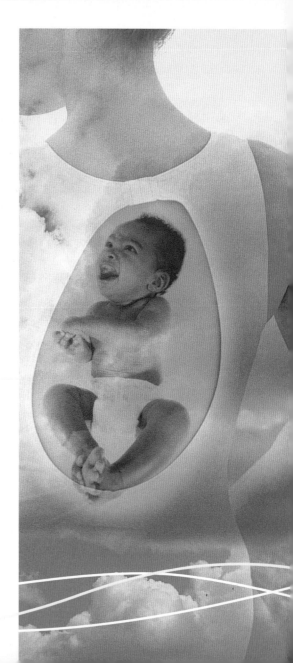

a difficult childbirth. This may be because her dreams have helped her to rehearse the birth experience and to prepare for it psychologically. Findings from a related study suggest that the more assertive you are in your difficult labor dreams, the shorter your actual labor will be, whereas if you feel victimized and powerless over the process in your dreams, your actual labor is more likely to be long.

Dreaming of your baby

Despite these findings, having a dream in which your baby appears is actually relatively rare. In only about 15 percent of your dreams are you likely to see your baby before childbirth. Even when you do dream of your baby, one study found that a woman cannot predict the sex of her child by using her dreams at any rate greater than that expected by chance. >

Dreams During Pregnancy

Expectant mothers' dreams change across their pregnancies. Researchers found that early in pregnancy, mothers-to-be dream of their babies easily being born or suddenly appearing without labor. As pregnancy progresses, mothers dream of birthing deformed babies or animals.

Late in pregnancy, mothers' anxiety about childbirth is directly revealed: dreams of a difficult labor become more frequent. Throughout pregnancy, women dream more often of their own mothers, and of buildings (reflecting changes in body size and body image).

Expectant fathers' dreams

What about the father? Do his dreams change during his mate's pregnancy? Researchers found that fathers' dreams show many of the same characteristics as do their mates'. Fathers-to-be dream more frequently of babies: of finding them, of them suddenly appearing, and of rejoicing in the birth.

Expectant fathers also show stage-related changes in their dreams. They dream more often of sex during the first trimester of their mate's pregnancy. These dreams may represent a desire by the father-to-be to return to the days in which he was free to have sex with a variety of partners. They may also show his sexual feelings are being threatened by the idea of fatherhood. Sexual dreams reassure the expectant father that he is still a sexual being and is still sexually desirable to others.

In the second trimester, just as the sexual dreams decrease in frequency, the father-to-be begins to dream more often of being protecting and loving toward his mate. He may be dreaming

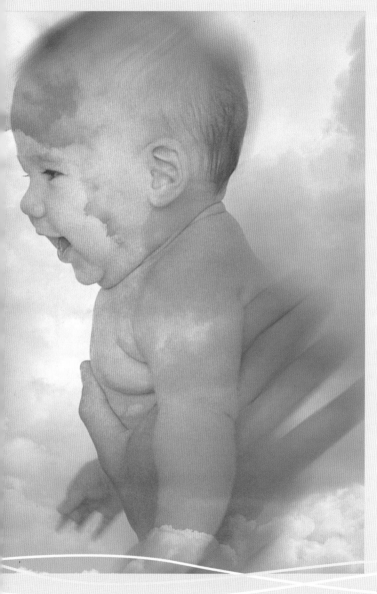

of his own childhood family as he considers what it means to be a father. As pregnancy progresses, an expectant father may actually dream of being the one to give birth—either as a wish to give birth or as a desire to save his mate from the pain of the experience.

The stereotype of men feeling excluded from their mate's pregnancy as it progresses shows up in their dreams. In one study, over 50 percent of expectant fathers dream themes of being isolated and excluded. Sharing dreams with your mate during this time can help each of you to feel more supported, valued, and understood.

Do my children have different kinds of dreams to mine?

Children's dreams were studied most completely in a sleep laboratory, where children slept, were awakened several times during the night, and were asked what they had just been dreaming about. These studies illuminated the way in which dreaming develops, and produced some fascinating findings about children's dreams.

How children's dreams change

Between the ages of three and five, children begin to report very short dreams. They dream most often of their bodies and of familiar animals and people. Small children's dreams are more static and bland than story-like; they don't mention feelings, interactions, or much activity.

At five- to seven-years-old, dreams become longer as REM periods physically lengthen. Children dream more often of people, some of them imaginary, and they introduce interactions and movement. Their storylines are simple, similar to the ones they might produce when asked to make up a story when awake.

Until the age of nine, children don't seem to dream very often, but by the age of nine, children's dreams become similar in length to those of adults. They have become narrative and storylike. Their

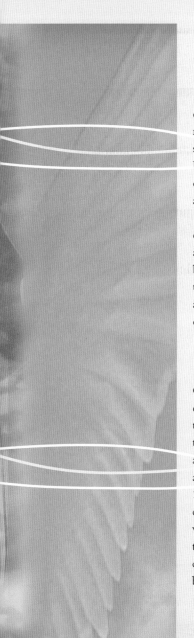

dream characters, mostly human now, have personalities, with some feelings and thoughts. Unlike adults, though, the most common feeling reported in this age group's dreams is happiness!

By the age of 13, young dreamers have more anger and apprehension in their dreams, and by 15, their dreams are essentially the same as adults' dreams, with apprehension being the most common dream emotion.

Children's dreams at home

Others have collected children's dreams which they reported to their parents at home. The dreams that children tell their parents are more violent and scary than adults' dreams. One study of 10,000 dreamers found that children who read scary books were three times more likely to have nightmares, and that children's dreams are more affected by reading than are adults'.

Children's Dreams

Ages 3–5:
Very short dreams of their bodies, people they know, and pets.

Ages 5–7:
Dreams lengthen a bit, more dreams of people (some unfamiliar), simple storylines.

Age 9:
Same length as adults', with narrative storylines. Characters have personalities.

Ages 13–15:
More negative feelings. By age 15, very similar to adults' dreams in every way.

What does it mean if I dream that I have had a baby, but I'm not a mother in waking life?

In my experience with clients, this kind of dream can feature human babies or animal babies, and occurs most often in two situations: either the dreamer is thinking about becoming a parent or of parenthood in general, and/or the dreamer is undergoing great change.

Planning for a baby

If you are considering having a child, baby dreams reflect those thoughts. They may also help you clarify your feelings about being a parent. Baby dreams serve to rehearse you for what may be a real, life-changing experience.

Transformation in its infancy

If you're not actively considering becoming a mother, and think that maybe the second explanation fits your current situation, you can ask yourself a series of questions to help you explore further. First, consider what the baby is like. Is there a new part of yourself, a quality, strength, or skill that is unfamiliar, that you are bringing into being right now? If so, think about where and how the dream baby was born and whether or not he or she

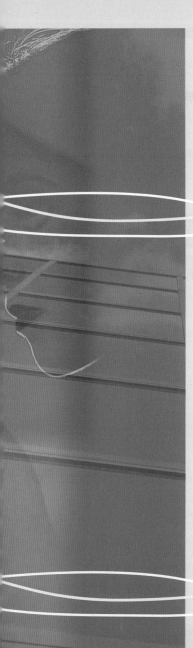

might reflect your experience with this new part of you.

Also ask yourself, is the baby healthy? Sickly? Starving? Well-nourished? Babies in dreams can indicate whether or not you are nurturing yourself, and how well.

How did the baby get here? Do you remember giving birth in the dream, or did he or she just appear? Perhaps the inner change you are going through is difficult; perhaps it is as simple as realizing it has already happened.

How old is the baby? Sometimes age will relate to how long the change in you has been in motion. For example, you might have ended your marriage three months ago and find yourself dreaming about a three-month-old baby—the new, fragile, single you.

Is the baby safe, or in need of protection from you, or someone you know? That might indicate that someone in your waking life environment is unable or unwilling to accept or care for the "new" you. Alternatively, you may just fear they will not accept you. If this is a person you trust, you might try talking to them about your feelings. Protecting your own vulnerable feelings is important, especially during times of transition and transformation.

Is the baby neglected, or are you attending to or even playing with it? This might give you information about how you unconsciously feel about the change in yourself. We tend to resist change somewhat in others and in ourselves, even when the change is positive. How well are you mothering yourself?

Even though I'm in my forties, I often dream of my childhood home. Is this unusual?

Not at all! Earlier and later in the night we dream of things from the far-distant past (see page 30). Many dream content studies demonstrated that most people dream about their childhood setting and family of origin throughout their lives. Often, we have those kinds of dream when something in the current situation is reminding us of something from the long-distant past.

Blending past and present

On those nights when you do have such a dream, consider whether your present circumstance seems familiar to you in some way. Think about your childhood as it was when you lived in the house you dreamed about. One way to help recall feelings from that time is to take a pencil in the hand you don't usually use to write with, and draw the floorplan of the house. Then label the rooms, still using your non-dominant hand. Being uncoordinated in such a basic way can help you feel the state of childhood, when you were small, when others were big, and every large person seemed to know more, and be able to do more, than you did.

>

Remember, too, that dreams are really about feelings. We can get caught up in intellectually interpreting our dreams and ignore the emotional state they express or portray. How did you feel in your dream? Is that feeling familiar to you?

Remodeling your psyche

Sometimes, you may dream you are exploring your own childhood home as an adult, and discover new rooms as the house has been remodeled. This is a common dream related by people in psychotherapy. As you will see in Part Two, houses can represent the psyche, and effective therapy can spark a "remodeling job" within it. As we mature and rely less on the coping strategies we used in childhood, our inner house can reflect that change. Our dreams can blend the childhood home with our current home to represent the very real situation within our own minds: some things have changed, some things have remained the same.

>

CONTINUED >

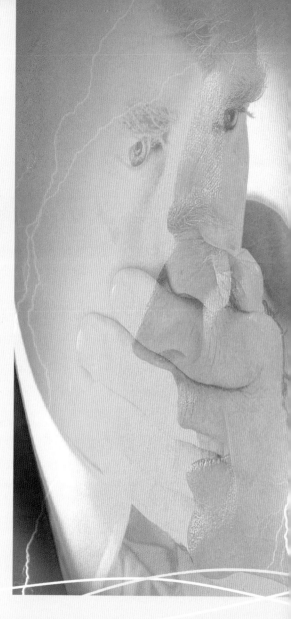

The world of work

Often we dream of co-workers, mates, or work situations set in our childhood homes. These kinds of dreams are very important, because they show us that we are questioning, or are confused about where we "are" in the world. We may even have the real people we work with unconsciously confused with our parents. Although the boss is obviously not mum or dad, we may expect him or her to behave that way. When we have strong feelings at or about work, and start dreaming of work and childhood blending, it may indicate such confusion. Are we back among those people we grew up with, meaning that we can justifiably expect them to behave as they did toward us back then? Or are we adults with completely different kinds of people? Or are both things true: the people we have surrounded ourselves with have some things in common with those people from childhood.

An example

For example, imagine you are a woman, and in waking life are having difficulty with your loved one, Charles. It seems to you that Charles is putting you down a lot, and you find yourself feeling very angry and unsure what to do about it. As a child, you fought endlessly with your older brother, Harry, who was a master of the sarcastic insult. One night, you have a dream set in your childhood house, in which Charles is living in Harry's room. Is Charles really as difficult as Harry was? And, more importantly, are you still the little girl you once were? Is Charles really treating you as if you were a child? In any case, you now have adult options—as long as you recognize that your feelings are left over from a time when you did not. Realizing that Harry and Charles are joined in your mind, you can now separate them, and have a frank talk with Charles about what kinds of comments are acceptable to you, and with Harry, too, about how his insults affected you when you were growing up.

My dreams seem so bizarre, sometimes I wonder if I'm crazy. Can you assess your mental health by looking at your dreams? Should I worry about my dreams?

Few studies have been carried out on psychiatric populations' dreams, mainly because those in mental hospitals are often taking medication that interferes with dreaming and recall. However, of the studies that have been done, the only consistently reliable difference found between the dreams of various diagnostic groups and "healthy" individuals has been for people with depression, schizophrenia, those suffering from post-traumatic stress disorder (PTSD), and those ceasing use of alcohol and other drugs. (In the latter group, nightmares and vividness increase along with the increase in dream recall once a person stops using the drug.)

Dreams of schizophrenics

Studies on chronic schizophrenics' dreams showed that their dreams differ from non-schizophrenics' dreams in that the former dream more frequently of women, and rarely have dreams in which friends appear, or any character is friendly. Striving for achievement is uncommon, as well. This probably reflects the isolation many people with

schizophrenia feel, and their hopelessness at overcoming their condition. Those with schizophrenia dream more of aggression with familiar people, and have more dreams with morbid death themes. Despite these findings, even experienced clinicians have difficulty differentiating the dreams of schizophrenics from those of other clinical groups.

*D*reams **and depression**
Clinically depressed people have shorter dreams, with less featured in them than do non-depressed people. Moderately depressed people have bland but unpleasant dreams, with few people in them, and those who do appear are most often family members and others from the past. Deeply

>

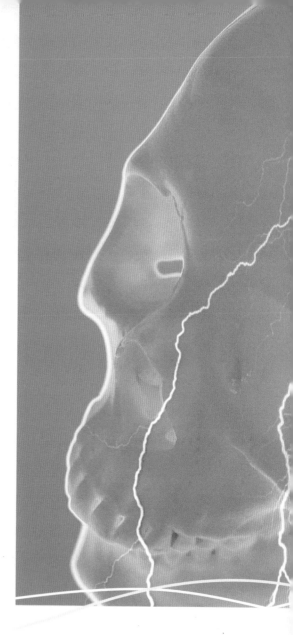

depressed people recall far fewer dreams than do other people, even in sleep laboratories. In their dreams, sufferers are typically alone, or with one other person rather than a group. Again, deeply depressed people dream more often of their family members.

However, depressed people also dream of happiness and friendly interactions more often than do the non-depressed. They tend to have escape dreams, in which they are going away from home, often on vacation. They also experience rejection in their dreams more frequently than do the non-depressed. However, because of the neurochemical changes that accompany both of these disorders, it is difficult to say what these dream differences mean psychologically.

Post-traumatic stress dreams

Although not everyone who suffers a trauma develops post-traumatic stress disorder, or PTSD, those who do develop it following a traumatic experience (including survivors of childhood abuse) tend to have more nightmares than do other people. In PTSD, the person relives the initial part of the horrifying event by feeling the same as they felt when it really occurred. A person with PTSD is susceptible to triggers that activate the feeling-based

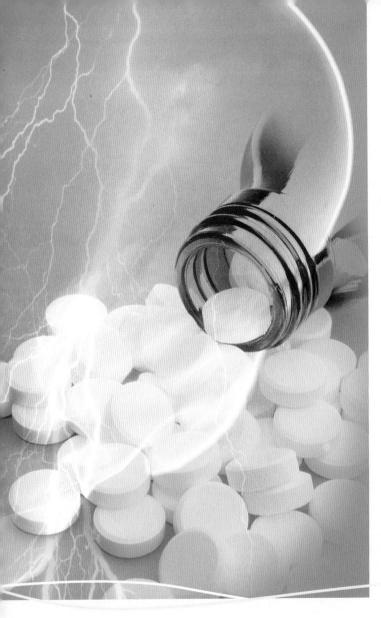

memory of the original trauma. Although people with PTSD know they are not physically back in the same situation, they *feel* as if they are. In nightmares, sufferers relive the feeling of the traumatic experience, which itself is replayed just as it was experienced, or with only slight distortion. Nightmares in PTSD often appear only after years have passed since the original trauma.

When to worry

If your dreams disturb you, and have been doing so for some time, please seek help to understand them. Other experiences and conditions can be responsible for each of these patterns in dreaming, though, so you would never diagnose a person by looking *only* at their dreams. If psychologists and dream experts cannot accurately do so, you shouldn't try it either!

What can be done about nightmares?

Who has nightmares?

Nightmares have many causes. Research suggests that most adults who have a lot of nightmares are more likely than others to remember their childhoods unusually well; to have more concerns about death than others; to have been sensitive children; and to have undergone no unusual traumas (the exception is childhood abuse, which is correlated with later life nightmares). Nightmare-prone people tend to have *"thin boundaries"*—that is, they are unusually affected by other people, are sensitive, and have difficulty defending themselves against painful feelings. Remember that most dreams—for everyone—are more unpleasant than pleasant, but truly fear-inspiring dreams tend to also be related to waking life trauma or daily tension.

Psychotherapists notice that their clients tend to have more nightmares when grieving and at other stressful periods during their therapy. Also, remember that many drugs (including alcohol and prescription medications) can cause nightmares.

Healing your night fears

Various techniques have been developed to help people reduce the frequency of their nightmares. Whether or not nightmares must be interpreted to be stopped is debated among dreamworkers. Several methods of working with nightmares seem to show that doing something with the nightmare is as effective, or more effective, than trying to find a reason for the dream or to tease out its meaning. (See pages 114–117 for help in stopping nightmares.)

>

Getting Back into the Dream

Each method for stopping nightmares begins with picturing yourself back in the dream. Because nightmares are, by definition, frightening dreams, it is important to ensure your own emotional safety while imagining any potentially upsetting situation. Don't work with a dream that elicits real terror, and if at any time you begin to feel uncomfortable, stop the process. Some people prefer to have a trusted friend nearby.

Before you begin, make sure you are in a quiet setting and unlikely to be disturbed. Some people perform rituals that help them to feel protected or centered. Lighting a candle before beginning and extinguishing it at the end is one way to make the boundaries of your dreamwork clear. You may also want to ask for protection and guidance, or say a prayer appropriate to your religion.

Sit quietly and focus your attention. Imagine yourself descending a staircase, and when you reach the bottom, you will enter the beginning of the nightmare. Once you can vividly imagine yourself there, you should easily be able to perform any of the techniques for stopping nightmares.

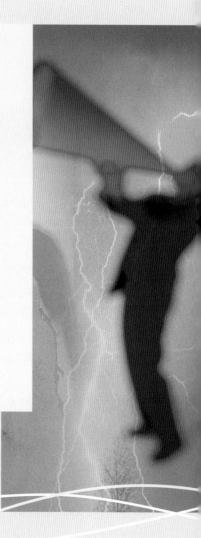

Behavior modification

Imagine yourself back in your dream. Replay the dream to yourself until just *before* the point when you start to feel scared. That may be very early on. Stop. Again, imagine the dream from the beginning until you start to feel scared. Stop. Use the relaxation techniques described on pages 70–71 to relax you. When you are ready to begin again, and staying as relaxed as possible, visualize the dream action going a little bit further. Stop as soon as you notice yourself becoming tense. Relax. Repeat this process until you are actually confronted in the dream with what frightens you. If you find yourself becoming tense or fearful while imagining, take a step back and don't go so far. Eventually (and this may take several days or weeks), you will be able to move calmly through the entire dream in your imagination. At that point, you've

reconditioned yourself not to respond with fear to the frightening element, and it has lost its power over you.

This technique is powerful for all kinds of relearning, and works even better if you reward yourself each time you take a step toward the feared element.

Be a curious hero

This method of working with nightmares begins at the point at which you face your dream enemy in your imagination, or when you feel the greatest fear if no enemy is actually present. Instead of doing what you did in the dream, try imagining yourself being a strong and fearless hero, with integrity and curiosity on your side. What is this scary dream element trying to do? Is it really trying to harm you? If so, why? What does it need or want from you? And who hired it to terrorize you in this way? Of

course, in reality, you did! You made it up. But why? Perhaps you are trying to show yourself something important.

Now, ask these same questions of your frightening dream element (if the element is not human, or even a creature, then you can still communicate with it—even doors can talk in dreams!). Display curiosity and willingness to understand. If your dream figure continues to be hostile, tell it something like, "I will not fight with you. If you have something you wish me to know, I'm listening. Otherwise, I'm just not interested," and end the exercise. For some people, this technique works best while writing, transcribing your own voice and the answers from the dream figure as dialogue. Don't worry if you feel you are "making up" the dream figure's answers. Just continue with the process. You might discover things about yourself you didn't know before.   >

CONTINUED >

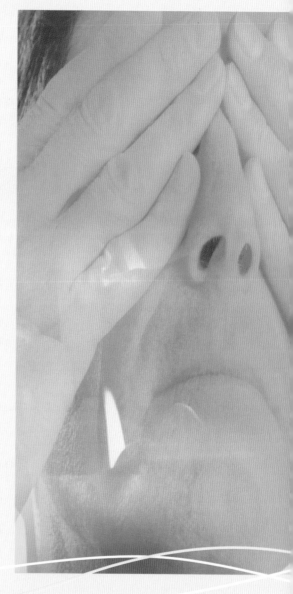

*R*elating the nightmare to current concerns
Harry Wilmer, who developed this technique to use
with Vietnam War veterans, found it helpful to work
with nightmare sufferers in a group. He asked what
the dream is trying to communicate that might help
the dreamer, how the storyline of the dream reveals
this, what current experiences are triggering the
dream, and how they are related to feelings
experienced in the nightmare. Group members
questioned the dreamer, asking him to clarify
elements in the dream. Then each member told the
dreamer what he thought the dream meant.
Sometimes the group used Gestalt techniques (see
pages 15–16) to re-enact the dream. Wilmer helped
the dreamers to see how their frightening
experiences were similar to those of warriors. Using
this larger mythological context, understanding the
daily real-life experiences being exaggerated in the
frightening dreams, and the experience of having a
supportive community with whom to express their
fears, led many dreamers to stop having the
nightmares that had plagued them for years. You
might try starting your own dream-sharing group,
or practice these ideas on your own.

Classic active imagination

Jungians have dreamers re-enter the dream in their imagination, and when they reach a dream image that seems important, focus upon it. If you feel afraid, try the exercise under "Behavior Modification" until you can focus on the image without fear. Your goal will be simply to focus on the scary image. Gradually, as you watch it, it will change. Observe these changes. It's very important not to consciously direct what evolves. Instead, allow the unconscious to present changes to the image. What the image changes into often provides important information about the original image, and frequently halts nightmares.

Fighting the enemy

This is a controversial technique that many dreamworkers feel is not necessary if you use the other techniques. In it, you destroy the enemy in your imagination. The problem with this method is that often the enemy returns in another form or under another guise to terrorize you again. If you use this technique, make sure you end your visualization with something positive coming from the destruction: flowers growing out of ashes, for instance.

Artistic expression

If you are uncomfortable interacting with your dream figures, expressing them in art can be very helpful. Just the act of getting them out of your head and into objective reality seems to heal many people's nightmares. Draw, paint, write a story, or make a collage or video of your frightening dream situation. If you want to, you can go a step further and show the dream situation changing to a positive outcome.

Ending the exercise

Once you've completed any exercise using your imagination, make sure you thank the dream elements you observed or interacted with. If you spoke with them, you might ask them if it is all right for you to visit them again. This communicates respect for the unconscious and makes it less likely that your dreams will again represent unknown aspects of yourself in such exaggerated, scary ways. Then, walk back up the stairway, knowing that when you reach the top, you are out of the dreamworld.

Dream Characters

WHAT DO THE PEOPLE and animals who populate your dream life really mean? In this chapter, you'll discover what religious or aggressive characters may signify, and how to safely meet your own dark side. People who turn into other people, or whose identity is uncertain, can be important messengers about your relationships. Read on to learn what the characters in your dreams can teach you.

What does it mean if I hurt or kill someone in my dream? Does it mean I want to injure or murder them when I'm awake?

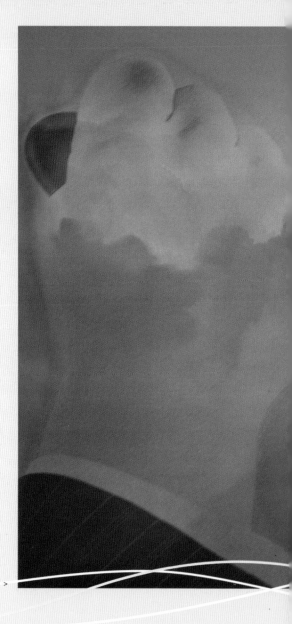

The History of Dream Research (pages 10–21) discussed the four major psychological dream theories. Each of these theories would have a different interpretation of a dream in which you kill someone. The Freudian and Jungian points of view are the most different from one another on this subject.

Freudian theory

Freudian (also called *psychoanalytic*) dream theory holds that this kind of dream may express a forbidden wish to remove the person (or the part of yourself that person represents) from your life. Your aggressive feelings are breaking through from your unconscious to your conscious mind and are symbolized in an attempt to keep them from disturbing your conscious mind too much. The person you kill in your dream may be just a stand-in for the person you are really angry at—often a parental authority figure.

Freudians also see dreams as representing unconscious fears. Looked at in this way, the dream may be saying that you are afraid that if you actually let this person know you are angry, it will be *as if* you have killed them (they will not survive it somehow, if only emotionally), or alternatively that you will lose control and actually kill them! Such a dream could give you more information about your emotional life. For instance, you may be a person who fears anger, feels it cannot be contained, or confuses anger and violence (which are, of course, two very different things). These beliefs are often learned as we are growing up, observing relationships around us.

Our experiences with authority in early childhood leave remnants in the psyche. Modern psychoanalysts, some of whom are called *object relations theorists* (a school of psychoanalysis begun in England in the mid–1900s), might say this dream illustrates a conflict going on entirely within your psyche. You may be trying to "kill off" or eliminate some part of yourself, perhaps an over-harsh parental figure you internalized in childhood.

All psychoanalysts would be interested in gaining your free associations to the dream. In free association, which is another method of examining your unconscious associations to various dream elements in an attempt to understand them, you are

encouraged to let your mind wander from the dream images. You might imagine your dream victim, writing down or tape recording what comes to you. This process may help you to discern the true identity of your victim. Since there are no symbols in this dream, you would not be able to interpret it from a Freudian perspective.

Jungian theory

A Jungian analyst might see this dream as a shadow dream. In it, you are a murderer. Your rage, lack of compassion, need for revenge, or whatever else fuels the killing, are unfamiliar to you in their intensity. You awaken and think, "Me? How could I do such a thing?"

Jungians describe dreams as being compensatory to waking awareness. In other words, what you know about yourself, you tend not to dream. What you don't know, and need to know,

you dream. If you have an exaggerated, one-sided attitude or feeling toward a situation or person in your waking life, your dreams will present the opposite point of view. It is as if the dream is saying, "Wait a moment. Your views are very extreme and out of balance." It then presents the opposite (unconscious) point of view in an attempt to balance your psyche and increase your awareness of yourself.

Jungians also feel that each of us has the potential to act in any way that humans act or have acted throughout history, given certain conditions. It is possible for each of us to feel murderous rage, although most of us don't act out those feelings in the physical world. Feeling angry is never bad, but actions to which anger can lead can be destructive, both to others and to ourselves. Feelings only become destructive when they are expressed in an unhealthy way, are unrecognized, >

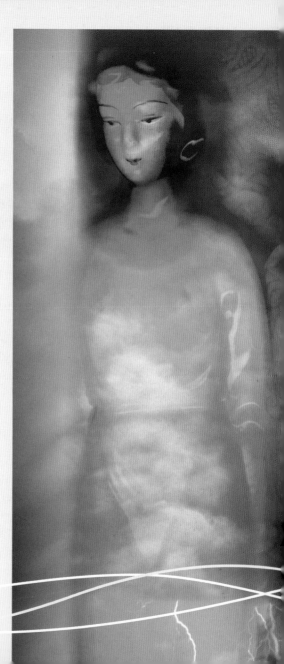

disowned, or denied. A dream of killing someone
may indicate that your anger has become out of
balance, exaggerated, and is not being tempered
by compassion.

It may also alert you to the way in which
you are "murdering" some aspect of yourself. In
other words, the person you kill could be a shadow
figure. If it is a stranger in the dream, the qualities
of yours the victim represents are farther away from
consciousness. If it is a familiar person, those
qualities are coming close to your awareness.

For example, let's imagine you are a man who
dreams (in a classic Freudian twist) of killing your
father. When you think about your father while you
are awake, you become annoyed at the way he
always seemed to want to control everything about
your family. You find that lately this quality is
something that is irritating you in many people, as
everyone seems so domineering and rigid. No one
just goes with the flow, allows others to be and is
accepting. This never bothered you much before, but
now, you can hardly stand to think about people
who are so controlling.

A preoccupation with such a strong feeling
suggests that, while awake, you are starting to see the
trait of being controlling as it appears in other
people. Soon, you may realize that you, too, have
this tendency that you have lately been projecting

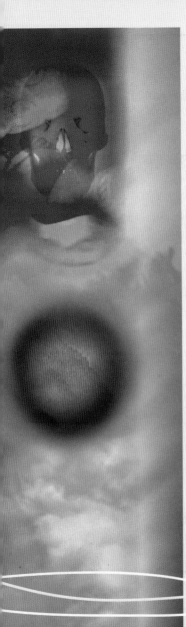

upon other people in an attempt to become aware of it within yourself; for we can only see in ourselves what we have first believed to exist in other people. As you begin to be aware of this quality, you may have a dream in which you are the controlling one. You may also start to recognize that although you are capable of being controlling, you are not your father. At that point, you are well on the way to integrating a former shadow quality. You can then decide when and where being controlling might be an asset.

There is a simple exercise you can do to illuminate shadow qualities that are coming closer to your awareness (see the box on page 127). Try identifying these, and then seeking them out in your dreams (especially among strangers, in particular threatening ones). Over time, watch your familiarity with these dream figures change until, eventually, you, yourself, are exhibiting their qualities.

The lesson of violent dreams

Whether your dream means you are angry at a real other person, at parts of yourself, are trying to sabotage some emerging quality of your own, or are being encouraged to recognize unknown aspects of yourself, use your dreams of hurting others as evidence that you are human. It is important to remember that we all have aggressive feelings toward other people. Sometimes, we have dreams in which we hurt them. Violent, aggressive dreams are very common in the dreams of people all over the world. They do not necessarily mean we intend to hurt these people when we are awake, or that we would do so if given the chance.

>

Me and My Shadow

Jung described the shadow as the archetype that represents all the personality qualities you believe you don't have, qualities you view both positively and negatively. However, traits aren't, in themselves, either good or bad. All traits are appropriate and important in certain contexts at certain times. For example, being called "stubborn" is not flattering, until you recall that it can be a virtue to be stubborn when being asked or forced to change a deeply held moral belief. Being "selfish" is another quality we typically think of as negative, but it is important to be able to be selfish when you are depleted. In order to be able to continue to nourish others, you must sometimes shut the world out and nourish yourself first.

Shadow qualities come into our awareness when we are either confronted about them by someone else, face a situation in the external world, or through our dreams, when that quality represents something we need to express or alter in order for our real selves to function more effectively. Jung wrote that the shadow is the seat of creativity; the more shadow qualities you become curious about and admit to yourself, the more energy you will have for creative pursuits. People who have done "shadow work" (i.e., have attempted to recognize "negative" aspects of themselves, acknowledge them, and work to temper or appropriately express them), tend to be comfortable people to be around. This is because they are less likely to focus on those qualities in you, hold themselves superior to you, and judge you accordingly.

If you want to know what qualities of your own might be shadow qualities, try the following exercise.

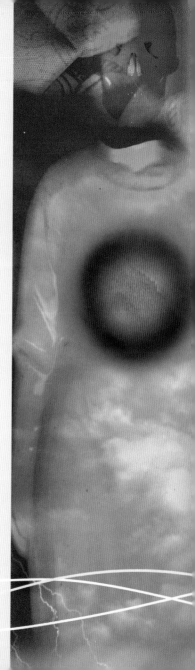

Discover your Shadow Qualities

Think of someone of the same sex as yourself whom you really admire. Then quickly list five or 10 admirable personality traits belonging to that person. Next, think of someone also of the same sex who really annoys you—you don't know why, but every time you think of, or interact with that person, you become irritated. Now list five or 10 of their annoying traits.

Take a deep breath and recognize that you've just listed qualities about your own self. Write down in what situation each of the annoying person's qualities could be a virtue. You may have to consider this for a while, or ask a friend for whom the quality is not a difficult one. Then spend some time thinking about how you could express the quality as a virtue. Make a commitment to yourself to play with those qualities during the next few days. Exaggerate them. Put on an act. Have fun!

The qualities you're admiring in that other person are also your own. You are looking at your own unknown face. Write a few lines of evidence that outlines when you have exhibited these very qualities. Become aware of these traits and honor them daily.

Repeat this exercise every couple of months, and watch your lists change. We are constantly becoming aware of the shadow, so the shadow is always changing. As we work with it, we gain a lot in our ability to understand and feel compassion for others and for ourselves.

I often have dreams where someone is chasing me, yet my life is not at all like that. What should I make of this?

The dream of being chased is among the most common of human dreams (see pages 76–77).

*T*he pursuer is you

Most dream theories view chase dreams in similar ways. Gestaltists might ask you questions similar to those in the box on page 129: what is chasing you is you, yourself. Jungians see these dreams as evidence that your own unconscious is trying to get your attention in an attempt to help you become aware of some important quality you may need to realize and express in your life at that moment. Whomever is chasing you is the personification, in the dream's visual language, of that quality or new version of yourself. Freudians might observe that you are fleeing from your own instinctual desires and impulses or fear retaliation from an authority figure (the pursuer).

Recall the last such dream you've had. Since this is a very common dream (being chased is the most typical kind of aggressive dream), you should be able to quickly remember one or two such dreams.

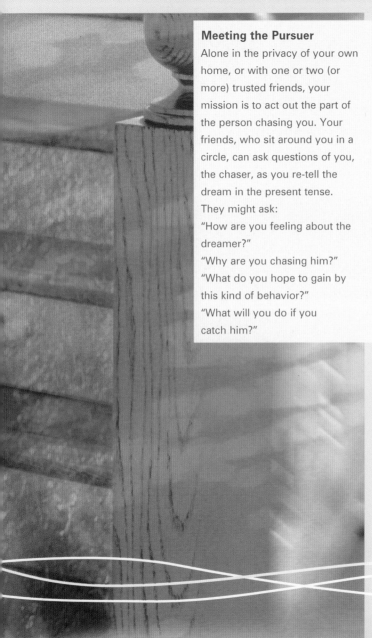

Meeting the Pursuer

Alone in the privacy of your own home, or with one or two (or more) trusted friends, your mission is to act out the part of the person chasing you. Your friends, who sit around you in a circle, can ask questions of you, the chaser, as you re-tell the dream in the present tense. They might ask:

"How are you feeling about the dreamer?"

"Why are you chasing him?"

"What do you hope to gain by this kind of behavior?"

"What will you do if you catch him?"

Then act out the part of yourself in the dream, telling the dream as if it were occurring now. Your friends could ask:

"Why are you running away?"

"Do you know this person is trying to hurt you?"

"What is your evidence?"

"What would happen if you stopped running, turned and faced your pursuer?"

"What are you so afraid of?"

"Is there anything else you could do besides run?"

"How do you feel about your pursuer?"

This exercise is remarkably illuminating when used with chase dreams. It can quickly become clear what parts of yourself are "split off" from your self-concept, and how threatening you may regard them as being. A conversation with your pursuer can lead to insights about how you run from yourself in daily life. Such insights might motivate you to make a change and express more of yourself.

If I dream about having sex with someone I'm not attracted to in real life, say a relative or a friend, do I secretly want to be with that person?

Maybe—maybe not. We've all heard that if you dream something, you really do want it to happen. That idea originally came from Sigmund Freud (see page 12), who later modified his views.

Some sex dreams *are* simple wish-fulfillment dreams: you want to be having sex with this fascinating, sexy dream person and when you wake up in the morning you try hard to get back to sleep in order to resume the dream.

Men's and women's sexual dreams

If you're a woman, sex dreams usually involve someone you know—your sexual partner, if you have one. Your feelings about the sexual experience in the dream can say a lot about your sense of the relationship. (See the box on page 133.) If you're a man, your sex dreams are more likely to involve someone you don't know well. Sometimes, these are clearly wish-fulfillment dreams, and can occur more frequently when you are between partners.

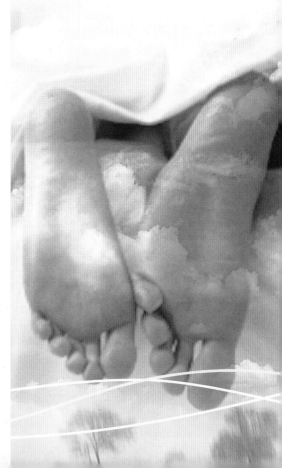

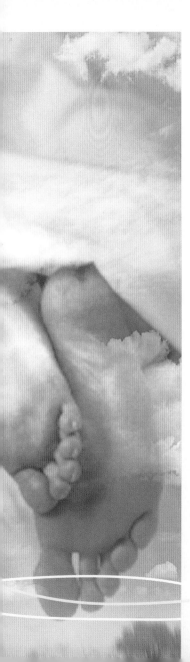

Most sexual dreams are full of apprehension and end badly. Men may have performance anxiety, and women, especially younger women, may dream of being caught, often by their parents. These fears mirror mostly unconscious waking life fears and attitudes about sexual expression. Both sexes fear interruption sometimes because they are about to awaken out of dreaming sleep.

Dreams of being raped are *not* considered sexual dreams! They belong under the category of violent dreams, and should be interpreted as such.

Sex and the self

Often erotic dreams aren't about sex as much as they are about your relationship with yourself. Having sex is the closest we can get to physically becoming one another. Psychologically, two people sexually uniting represent two sides of the self joining and becoming integrated—the conscious self, or ego, of the dreamer (one's sense of identity; see page 15) combining with one's unconscious, unknown personality. A sexual dream can mean that you've "let in" a previously unknown quality of yourself, and in so doing, changed your self-concept. What is your dream sex partner like? Using the first words that enter >

your mind, how would you describe this person? Consider whether or not these are qualities of your own that you have not yet recognized within yourself.

Whether you are having dream sex with a man or a woman is also important, as you'll see from the answer to the next question.

Why do I Want You so Much?

I teach a very large undergraduate course on sexuality at the University of California in Santa Cruz. Each year, I use several of the exercises in this book with my students, which they always find illuminating and enjoyable. This one can help you to understand why you feel such a strong attraction for someone.

Ask the following simple question about a dream character you are sexual with. (You can also ask it about a real person you are wildly attracted to.)

What qualities of this person do you most admire and would you most like to have for yourself?

Sometimes we are attracted to—and get involved with—sexual partners because we wish to become more like them. Thus trying on their characteristics before getting involved with them will help you determine the basis of your feelings for them. Some say answering this question and then striving to express that quality in your own life reduces strong, overwhelming attraction.

Uncovering Your Sexual Dreams

Look through your dream journal until you find a sexual dream or dreams that involve your partner. If, in the dream, your partner changes into—or is confused with—someone else, use the information on pages 142–143 to learn more. Otherwise, ask yourself the following questions:

• Is your partner acting the way he usually acts in real life? If not, is he acting like someone else you have known in the past?

• How do you feel in the dream: excited, afraid, nervous, aroused, guilty, ashamed, or happy? (Usually, sexual dreams are unpleasant, so don't be concerned if yours are, too. See pages 41, 62–63 for more information about feelings in dreams.)

• Are the emotions you experienced in your dream similar to feelings you have about your relationship during your waking life? Or are they leaking in from the past in some way?

• If someone you know well told you this dream, what would it make you think about their sexual relationship? Sometimes looking at a dream from a third person's point of view (even if you're just pretending to be that person) can clarify the message.

• Often, a couple's sexuality mirrors the emotional issues between them in other aspects of their relationship. Does the sex in your dream feel easy, comfortable, or safe; or controlled, restrained, and inhibited? Are you afraid you're

going to be "discovered" by someone else (which might indicate you fear your parents, past loves, or society at large may be acting as imaginary judges of your behavior in your own mind)?

• If dream sex with your partner is other than how you wish it would be, honor your dreams and yourself by talking with them about it. You can open the discussion by saying something like, "You know, I had this dream where we were having sex. I love how close we are when we are sexual with each other. Yet, in the dream, you seemed so distant. Do you ever feel that way?" Placing the discussion within the context of the dream makes it less threatening.

I've had dreams where I'm enjoying sex with someone of the same sex as myself. Does this mean I am homosexual or bisexual?

No! Most people have had these dreams. Many young people, especially, are concerned that if they dream of having sex with someone of the same sex, they are gay. I've had a few clients who were confused for years. They were attracted to and fell in love with women, but had dreams about men. This confusion is not limited to heterosexuals who are concerned they might be gay; I've also known gay men and women who have heterosexual dreams and fear that this means they are secretly straight. Again, sex dreams are often about the self (in this case, masculinity and femininity), not so much about sexual orientation.

Archetypal dream lovers

Some sexual dreams are archetypal. The archetypes that appear in erotic dream encounters are the anima and animus (see pages 14–15). The anima represents our feminine qualities, and the animus, our masculine; we all have both. Most women act out their feminine qualities in their lives; that is, they are more feminine. Therefore, their animus (masculine side) is more unconscious, and they

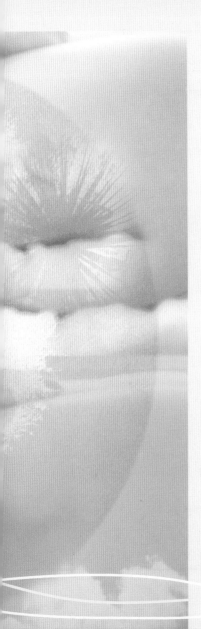

dream about having sex with masculine characters. Most men embody their masculine side in their waking lives, so their anima is more unconscious; their sexual dream encounters are therefore with feminine characters.

Whatever is unconscious has a tendency to be projected onto other people in the world, so one way to describe a man falling in love is to say he is projecting his own anima. At first, he doesn't really know the person he falls for. He imagines her as he would like her to be—an image of the ideal feminine in his unconscious. He is, essentially, admiring and falling in love with his own unknown self. The task of love is to unmask the archetypes so you get to discover who your lover really is underneath the image you've pasted over her. Only then can you know, and truly love her. (For an exercise that helps you meet your feminine or masculine image, see the box on page 137.)

In dreams, we can be presented with an almost pure image of our own unconscious masculine or feminine qualities and then, if we're lucky, we get to make love to it. The dream vision really is more of an "it" than a "who." No real person in the world can match your ideal image, but real people are so much more complex, fresh, and alive than an image could ever be

Gender role twist

Now, here is the twist: masculine women will meet the anima, and feminine men, the animus. In their dreams, these women might >

have sex with women (or very feminine men), and men might have sex with men (or very masculine women). This can also happen, for instance, if a man goes through a period where his emotions are at the forefront (such as after a loss or other major life transition). The dream is saying to such a man, "through this experience in the outside world, you are allowing yourself to get close to your feminine side." Confusing isn't it? Just remember that the anima and animus refer to gender, not biological sex.

A "big" dream (see page 13) that contains the anima/animus image is a very important dream. Jung wrote that because the anima/animus are so far from consciousness, so "not-me," they can act as guides to one's own soul. Meeting this archetype sexually in a dream is therefore a signal that you are beginning to meet with a deep part of yourself.

Frightening sexual encounters

Most commonly, such dream encounters are very positive, but sometimes they are not, for example when the anima/animus figure seems threatening or sexually dangerous. These dreams can occur in psychotherapy, when a client is working through sexual assault or childhood molestation. Using the techniques in the box on pages 114–117 for working with nightmares can help end fearful, sexual dream encounters.

Learning about your own unknown masculine or feminine qualities will help you understand what kinds of people you are likely to be attracted to. We tend to seek out and form relationships with people who represent these same qualities. Try the visualization exercise opposite.

Meeting Your Unconscious Feminine or Masculine Self

This is a visualization exercise that works best if you either read it through first and memorize it, or tape it and play it back to yourself. Close your eyes and relax, imagining yourself in the following scene:

You are walking on a wide path through a quiet forest at twilight. This is a safe, beautiful and perfect place, with light filtering through the trees. Feel the forest floor sink slightly beneath your feet with each step, releasing the scent of pine. Birds gently call to one another, rustling the branches overhead. Soon, you come to a white building with a massive, beautifully carved stone door. Walk toward it. You know that when you enter you will be greeted by your ideal romantic partner; someone you have imagined all your life; someone you have never met before. Take a deep breath. Place your hand on the doorknob and open the door. Who do you see waiting for you there? Take a long, close look. Once you've recovered from the physical perfection of your ideal love, ask yourself what kind of person this is. Stay as long as you need to in order to get a sense of this person.

Then, return to your present surroundings and slowly open your eyes.

You have just visualized the archetype of the anima or animus—your own unconscious feminine or masculine qualities. Now, describe the traits of the anima or animus. You might find some of them are contradictory, so cannot exist in the same person (part of the reason relationships can be so frustrating). Do you recognize this person from your dreams? If not, for the next several nights, watch your dream world for sexual dreams, as you've just invited the anima or animus to appear! Then note what traits this character displays. If you were this character, how would you see the world? What decisions would you make? How would you express your values and spirituality? The anima/animus is the archetype that can lead you to discover your soul.

I have a recurring dream that my husband and I are making love. It is a very erotic dream, but the odd thing is, he has no face! What could this mean?

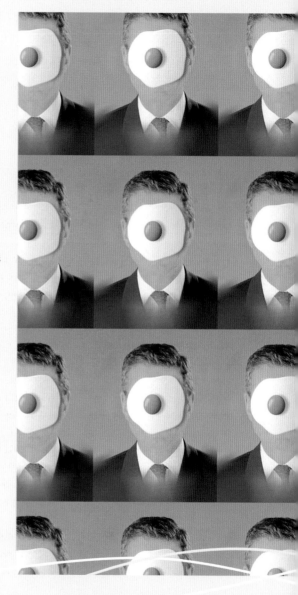

Recurring dreams demonstrate that the unconscious is trying to find its way out of a difficult problem. Many people have recurring dreams for years that don't change at all. Others have recurring elements in their dreams, or dreams in which a single theme recurs, although the individual dreams change. Treat all recurring dreams as important dreams.

*Q*uestions to ask

What is the problem your unconscious is trying to solve? Only you can answer that question, but some possibilities to think about are listed below. Remember that there are many possible meanings to most dreams. The faceless lover dream is no exception:

• You might be feeling guilty about your sexuality, and the only way to have a pleasurable experience would be with someone you don't really see, so you

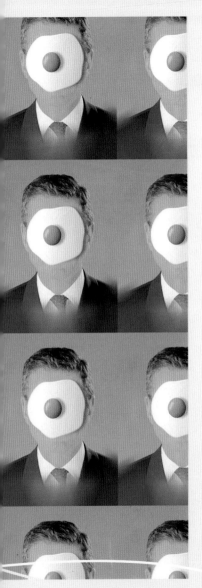

make your husband into a faceless stranger.

• Your unconscious beliefs about marriage may not include the possibility of wild, sexual abandonment—many people's don't! So sex can only be great if it's not with your husband.

• The dream may be picturing a real emotional situation: you may realize you do not really know your husband. He may recently have said or done something that made him feel like a stranger to you. Of course, it takes a lifetime to *really* know another person, so the dream may just be illustrating that fact to you.

• Alternatively, you may feel your husband doesn't really know you. If he has no face, he has no eyes, and therefore he can't really see you.

• Your dream husband may represent a part of the animus that is unknown within you (see pages 14–15 and 137)—in this case an erotic and active sexuality.

• You may be afraid of being emotionally intimate with someone you are also sexual with. This is a common fear, especially among younger people.

• Such a dream may indicate that you are not connecting with the more "base," body-oriented, sexual part of your husband. That when you have sex, you perceive him split into his sexual body and the person you know.

Sometimes I dream that I am not a character in my own dream. They have a curious quality—rather than being a participant, I am observing the action.

As the observer of all of the action in your dreams—the dream "camera"—your sense of yourself in the dream is the *dream ego*. In dreams where you are an observer and not even a character or participant, the dream ego can be easily felt. The entire time that you are dreaming, a part of yourself is observing the creation of your mind. It is commenting upon the action, sometimes questioning what is happening.

From a safe distance

Several experts hold that the content of dreams in which you are an observer is more threatening to your conscious mind than that of dreams in which you are a participant. Whatever you are observing is placed at a distance to you, one more step from reality. Not only is this a dream, but you're not even in it. You therefore are not likely

to have the same feelings you would if you were a character in the dream, so if the dream is too painful or frightening, you are less likely to awaken from it. Instead, you watch what happens from a safe, protected distance.

Dreaming of dreaming, plays, movies, TV

Sometimes you may dream that you are dreaming, and wake up into a dream. Sometimes you dream you're starring in a movie. These are variations on the same theme. In each case, the dream is saying, "this is absolutely not real, don't get upset, it's not only just a dream, it's a dream within a dream and at the base level, it's just a movie, anyway!"

Dreams with films and television in them can be examined more closely as projection dreams. What is going on inside the television show or film is most threatening of all at the moment, and can represent a quite clear "projection" of your own unconscious. What "old movie" is yours showing you?

Sometimes I have dreams where one person changes into another. For example, my husband changes into an ex-boyfriend, or my mother changes into my sister. What does this mean?

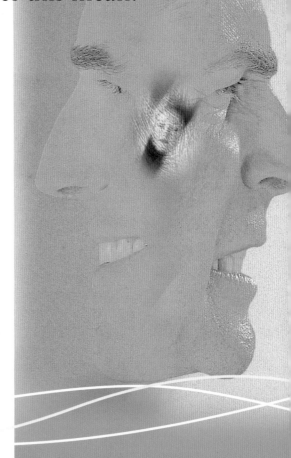

These dreams are called *metamorphosis* dreams (*condensation* in Freudian dream interpretation), and most people have had dreams in which someone changes into someone else. In other kinds of metamorphosis dream, you might be unsure who a character really is: one person seems to be someone else, and then also themselves. Often, these dreams occur early on in new friendships or romantic relationships, when you are just getting to know another person. You have invested your feelings in the relationship, and are understandably watchful lest this new person turn out to be similar to someone you've interacted with before. This pattern can easily be imagined if you've been hurt in past situations. You don't want to feel that pain again, so your unconscious is protectively on the lookout for potential similarities between the person who hurt you and the new person.

Consider, for instance, the following dream from Anne, a woman in her 30s, who began dating Tom a few months ago. Jack is her last boyfriend.

"I realize with horror that I have been dating Jack again, not Tom. But then I am talking to Jack, and suddenly realize he is not Tom. I say to myself, Tom has tanner skin than Jack. We are in my house. Jack has moved in; his food is in my kitchen cupboards. I know I have to tell Tom goodbye, because he is really Jack, and I know Jack is not good for me. I am very sad about this. Yet I question whether or not Tom is really Jack. This is very confusing."

Anne is understandably bewildered. How can she tell who is who? Although Tom and Jack look different from one another, Jack has "moved in." Recall that houses in dreams often represent the psyche (see page 104). Because metamorphoses in dreams signal confusion in the unconscious, it seems that Anne is concerned about whether or not Tom is really similar to Jack underneath ("not good for me"), and if their relationship will progress (and end) the same way. Yet, she also seems to know that Tom and Jack are different and feels sad at the idea of ending the relationship.

Confusion like this can happen when we displace our feelings for one person onto another person, especially when the new person is someone we don't know well. When displacement occurs, it's hard to tell who is who. Should Anne expect Tom to behave as Jack did? Or, in doing that, is she mistrusting Tom, unable to see who he really is?

Using metamorphosis dreams

How could Anne solve her dilemma? By realizing just how confused she is, she might take some time to learn more about Tom before deciding whether or not to leave him, especially since, in the dream, that plan makes her sad. She could also compare and contrast Tom and Jack's behavior, asking herself, "What would Jack have done in this situation? What is Tom doing now?," making lists of Tom's and Jack's traits and evidence in their behavior for each trait, asking Tom questions about himself and his past relationships, progressing slowly toward emotional intimacy, and seeking trusted friends' opinions about Tom. All of these information-gathering methods would help Anne to determine whether her fears about Tom are founded in present reality, or more appropriately belong to a situation in her past that should be put to rest. They also suggest that Anne might benefit from grieving the loss of her relationship with Jack.

I had a dream about a religious figure. Do these kinds of dreams have any special significance?

Religious or spiritual dreams can feel so meaningful. Let's look at what each of the major psychological theories (see pages 10–21) would have to say about them, and then we'll consider what they might mean spiritually.

Freud and religious dreams

First, Freud wrote that religious figures in dreams reflect the image of one's parents in early childhood. The deity one believes in has many of the same characteristics as one's most dominant parent. We are familiar with that kind of ultimate authority figure from when we were little children, so we unconsciously believe the deity is a kind of expanded version of that person. If our parents were unusually punitive, we are more likely to believe in a religious system that has clear-cut rules and severe punishments. If our families were more egalitarian, the religion we adopt as adults is more likely to be equally so.

Freud described how we are born all *id*—we have only instinctual drives at birth, and they clamor to be expressed and satisfied. Next, we develop the *ego*—our sense of self, the part of the mind that is

rational and strives to get our id desires met as efficiently as possible. Finally, the *superego*, or internal moral authority, develops. It is initially identical to our parents' values, and its job is to remind us what is right and wrong, and to ensure we behave in a way that will win others' love.

How does this relate to dreams of religious figures? For Freud, these are representations of our superego. They illustrate the moral code we grew up under, internalized into our psyches, and now live by. Dreaming of a religious figure might mean you have recently done, or are about to do, something that either troubles your conscience, or something that would make your superego proud. If you have such a dream, examine your feelings of guilt and pride in your life at the moment.

>

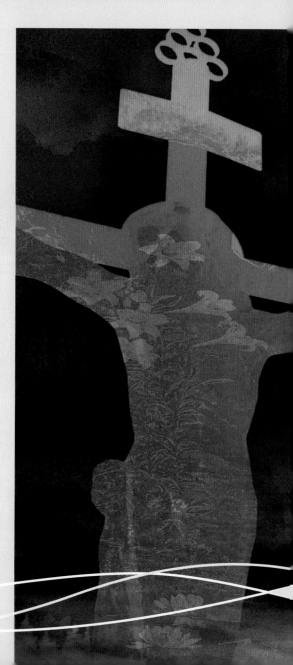

Archetypal religious dreams

Jung, however, wrote that religious figures represent
the self, the archetype of wholeness. Religious
figures in dreams point to the present possibility
of becoming a whole, integrated person, living out
your real self in the world. Depending on the
dream's content, the religious figure might appear
to show you that you are somehow being false to
yourself, have lost your way. Alternatively, he or she
may signal that you are on the right path.

Transitions

In psychotherapy and at other transitional stages,
people have dreams of religious figures undergoing
difficult times. In the United States, those dreams
are often of Christ being crucified. Sometimes
the dreamer will be a Christ figure, enacting the
passion. Such dreams tend to occur at particularly
painful times in development, when you realize that
a deep sacrifice in your outer life may be necessary
to preserve or express your real self.

Gestalt expression

A gestalt group might work with such a dream by
asking you to enact the religious figure, to describe

what he or she is feeling and thinking. Because all parts of the dream are you, the group would encourage you to consider the ways in which you are being crucified in your present waking life, and by which part of your psyche. Do you have a Herod or executioner inside who is keeping you from expressing your real needs and desires, strengths and weaknesses? What could you do to protect yourself, or to overcome it?

Phenomenology

Finally, phenomenologists, who don't interpret the meanings of dreams, would take this dream at face value: you are like this religious figure at this moment, undergoing the same experiences in your inner life.

The gift of religious dreams

Of course it's impossible to know for sure whether or not a religious dream is about your own psyche, something larger than yourself, or is a message from the one you are dreaming about. Many people, though, have found comfort and renewed hope in religious dreams during difficult times, while others have awakened with a new sense of strength and purpose.

Are animals in dreams, or creatures that are part-human or even inhuman, important?

Many dream experts from a Jungian or Gestaltian viewpoint treat dream animals and creatures as aspects of the self that are farthest away from awareness, whereas Freudians see them as symbolizing sexual and aggressive instincts. From the studies done on pregnant women's dreams (see page 95), we know that animals are certainly used as symbols. Jungians describe them as representing shadow aspects of ourselves (see page 126), which may either be admired, or disowned (and are therefore threatening in our dreams). Are you aware of what a cute, cuddly rabbit you are? Or what a wild and focused tiger you can be?

Spirit guides

In Native American spirituality, animals are extremely important. Viewed as spirit guides, each represents specific strengths (see Part Two for more). Shamans have an animal as a guardian spirit, which identifies itself to the shaman by appearing in three

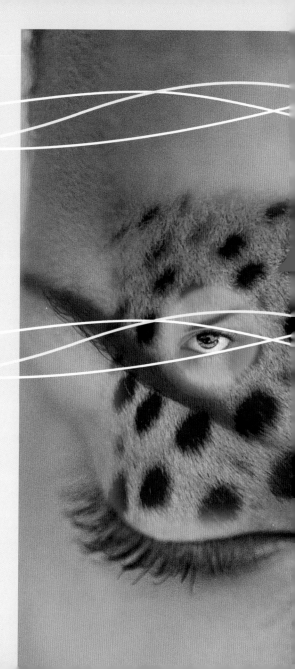

QUESTIONS AND ANSWERS

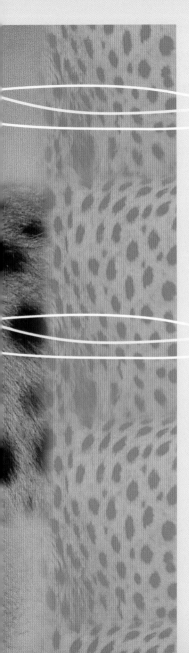

dreams. That animal then brings its particular quality to the dreamer whenever it is dreamed about. The shaman identifies with the animal, and may adopt its name. He or she feels a special relationship with the animal at a soul level, and may sense protection from it.

Inhuman creatures

Creatures that are wholly inhuman are rare in adults' dreams. In my experience, they occur when a person is feeling "inhuman," either from overwork or an over-reliance on the thinking function—that part of the personality which makes decisions solely based on logic and fact. Needing to do that on a regular basis at work, for example, can lead us to feel like a machine. Such a feeling may be portrayed in dreams of human machines and indicates a need for the dreamer to get back in touch with his or her emotional life and experiences of the natural world.

Is the way that your dreams end important?

Yes! One revealing way of exploring how achievement-oriented you are, and how successful you feel in the world, is to simply count up the number of times your dreams end with a success, failure, or unknown outcome. Do you try and win? Try and fail? Not try? Try and never know what will happen next? If there is a conflict in the dream, is it resolved by the end? Does this mirror what happens in your waking life?

*D*ream resolutions

Often, we'll have different dreams in which the same problem arises. Each dream will end without a resolution and when we wake up we feel frustrated. Sometimes, though, we will overcome the dream obstacle. If you have a dream like that, consider what you did in the dream to solve the problem. Did it work? Can you do the same thing in your waking life?

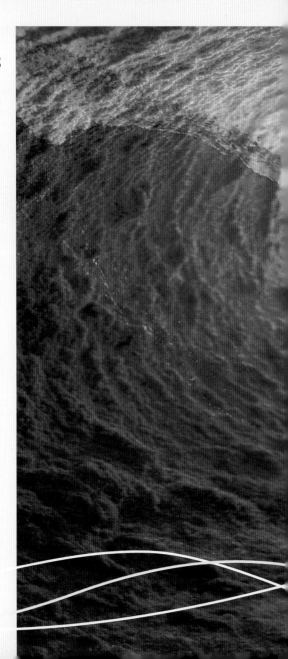

Next, consider the hedonic or feeling tone of the dream when it ends. Does it finish happily, or is there a dark and foreboding feeling at the end? Does the dream feel confusing when you wake up? Dreams that end with a feeling and no clear result might indicate that the resolution of the problem lies in attending to the feeling, or that the problem is the feeling!

Unusual and "Paranormal" Dreams

THIS CHAPTER WILL SEPARATE fact from fiction about dream telepathy and precognition, and will give you some techniques for using lucid dreaming and dream control to interact creatively with your dream world. You'll discover what dreams of the dead, end-of-the-world dreams, and recurrent dreams have to offer. Finally, you'll learn the answer to the question, "If I die in my dreams, will I die in my life?" (No!)

$\mathcal{D}$o dreams ever tell the future?

The scant research on dreams of the future that later come true (called *precognitive* dreams) is inconclusive. Nevertheless, in my psychotherapy practice, I am impressed when my clients come in with a dream one week, and then elements from it occur in their lives the following week. Some of these instances could be explained by the dreamers working on a problem in their therapy and unconsciously imagining in a dream the solution they are about to become aware of consciously. People who are concentrating intensely on a person or situation often have insights or intuitions about it that first find their way into dreams. Psychotherapists notice that the unconscious, as it shows itself in dreams, seems to be three to six months ahead of most people's waking consciousness.

$\mathcal{E}$erie coincidence

Even if much of the time these dreams can be explained by insight or intuition without needing to believe in precognition, now and then the seemingly predictive qualities of dreams can be eerie. One client of mine, originally from New York City, came to her session in early September 2001, just before I was about to leave on my vacation. She reported to me a dream she had had the night before:

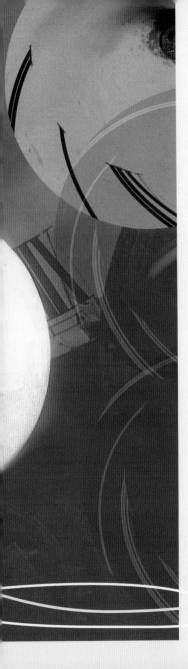

"I am in a large building in Manhattan. It is very tall, a skyscraper, but it has no interior walls, so when I look up, I can see the ceiling far away. There are many people working there, as there would be. Suddenly the walls start to melt. I am confused. I try to find the door. There is fire. I have to get out. I wake up."

I immediately wondered whether or not this dream was triggered by my impending vacation, yet it didn't seem like a typical fear of abandonment dream. Neither of us knew then what would happen less than a week later in New York.

There are so many similar elements between this dream and the tragedy in New York that it seems to be a typical precognitive kind of dream. Yet, the dreamer doesn't say, "I dream I am in a skyscraper in New York, and terrorists crash a plane into it."

Because studies have found that precognitive dreams tend to lack or distort details, it is hard to study them in any systematic way. Nevertheless, we are struck with the feeling that this dreamer sensed the events that were about to occur.

Anecdotal precognitive dreams

There are many anecdotal accounts of precognitive dreams, including those that predicted disasters such as the sinking of the Titanic. Researchers at Duke University's Parapsychology Laboratory collected hundreds of reports of precognitive dreams. Studies on such reports find that death is the most popular theme (50 percent) followed by accidents or injuries. Death, accidents, and injuries in which a close relative is the victim make up about half of all >

CONTINUED >

precognitive dreams. We don't know how often people dream of their loved ones dying or being hurt when it doesn't then happen in the real world, but the fact that people do seem to dream of these events in such remarkable ways does make one wonder.

Dream telepathy studies

Many intriguing dream studies have investigated people trying to predict, in their dreams, images being focused upon by another person at various physical distances from the dreamer. In nine of 13 well-designed studies, researchers found statistically significant results. In other words, dreamers dreamed of the sender's chosen image at a rate greater than that explained by chance.

I once participated as the "sender" of an image at an Association for the Study of Dreams (ASD) yearly conference in Santa Cruz. None of the attendees at the conference had ever been to my house, so I chose an image in a photograph on my wall of a woman doing an ancient form of hula on the beach. Potential psychic dreamers were to simply go to sleep, dream, and then write down their dream, while I was to stay awake all night, concentrating on the image at regular intervals. I told no one about the image. The next day, from the

universe of images I could have chosen, one person described the hula dancer image almost exactly. It had appeared in his dream during the night.

Have you ever dreamed of something occurring to another person at exactly the time it actually ended up happening? Jung described, in his autobiography, *Memories, Dreams, Reflections*, one such dream he had of his wife's cousin's death. Like precognitive dreams, I believe such telepathic dreams most often involve unexpected death or danger to another. I have heard so many of these dreams over the past 15 years of doing psychotherapy it feels unwise to dismiss them out of hand.

Déjà vu dreams

Many people feel they have just had an experience that they previously dreamed about without having remembered the dream until the experience triggers it. This is actually not precognition. It is a phenomenon that can be explained by the way the brain works, as sometimes our brains are delayed in processing incoming stimuli. We experience the event as having already occurred, and then (commonly called *déjà vu*), we get the feeling we know exactly what's going to happen next, and it does! What's really happening is that your brain processing is lagging behind input from your sensory receptors (eyes, ears, nose, etc.), so that although you've already experienced an event, you don't know it. Occasional *déjà vu* experiences are normal, but if this happens to you very frequently, please see your physician as it can be a sign of a disorder you need to investigate.

I have been having dreams about the end of the world. My friends have too. Should we be concerned?

People have been dreaming about the end of the world throughout history, and yet (thankfully), the world is still here. Remember that dreams have both an inner and an outer meaning.

Outer meaning

The outer meaning is the extent to which the dreams portray or are concerned with our actual, waking lives. The world is unstable. Political changes and threats are frightening. Although it is actually rare for people to dream about social ills, dramatic and violent events may find their way into our dreams. If you have an end-of-the-world dream, ask yourself if you are consciously allowing yourself to feel the feelings evoked in the dream. In such uncertain times, fear and hopelessness can take over.

Inner meaning

End-of-the-world dreams are considered to be archetypal dreams, and most dream experts agree that an end-of-the-world dream signals a major change in the dreamer's self. Your psyche may be saying to you, "the old way is ending and the

>

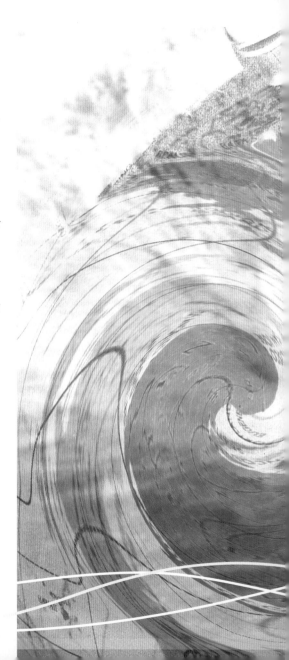

change is so complete, it is as if the familiar world is gone." It can take months or years after a major, life-changing event or transition for you to consciously realize the extent of that change.

oss

Major life transitions (birth of a child, divorce, career changes, marriage, financial success) and tragedies (loved ones hurt or lost) throw us into the stages of grieving described so well by Elizabeth Kubler-Ross. Even positive events can require us to change, and in changing, we gain as well as feel loss. Each of us, when facing a loss, travels through shock, denial, anger, bargaining, sadness/hopelessness/despair, and finally, acceptance. We move through these feelings in a spiral, feeling the loss more deeply each time, until we have become able to accept it. When the loss is the old self, it can be even more difficult to get through denial. At first, it is hard to really know you've changed on the inside if things look the same on the outside. Denial is a necessary and important part of change; you adopt it as a defense against what would otherwise be overwhelming anxiety. Your psyche needs time to absorb the loss, and it cushions itself by using denial.

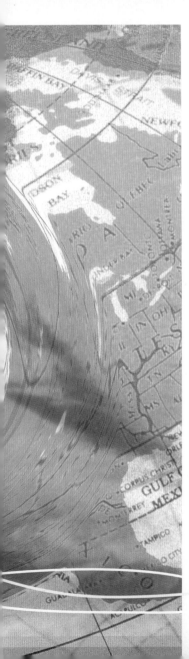

Change

Many end-of-the-world dreams occur when you have passed through the denial stage, and recognize emotionally that the loss did take place. Others happen when the life change is up ahead, and you are just becoming aware of it. Most people who have end-of-the-world dreams can describe the change that the dream represents. You may not know what to do with the change, or what might come after the change, but your dreams can help illuminate those answers for you. As with all "big" dreams, studying the elements within the dream (see the Dream Directory) and using the imaginal techniques on pages 114–117, 129, and 137 can help you to unlock the personal meaning of these dreams.

Uncertainty

Collectively, we are living in uncertain times; although of course that phrase would have also been appropriate to many phases in history. We possess the technology to destroy ourselves, so the end-of-the-world dream is not at all far-fetched. In uncertain times, news stories about possible ends to the planet seem to proliferate and get our attention. Although pollution, asteroids, the threat of nuclear war and accidents, terrorism, plague, and so on, have existed for decades, at certain periods of societal fragility we seem to be bombarded by them in the media, and fear rises in the general population. Overexposure to these stories can make people preoccupied with them, and they start to have end-of-the-world dreams.

The positive outcome of such dreams might be that we each consciously realize we are living in a challenging and dangerous time, instead of denying the reality of just how fragile our world is, and how much tending and respect it needs.

What if I dream about someone who has died? Does that mean that person is trying to communicate with me?

No one can answer this question with certainty, for it is a question of belief in the soul and its ability to survive bodily death. As no one really knows what happens when we die, such belief is a form of faith.

Many people dream of departed loved ones. I've noticed that my clients dream in fairly predictable stages about people who have unexpectedly died. These are similar to the stages of dreaming experienced by people who have suffered any kind of trauma. (If your loved one was ill and the death was not unexpected, you will have begun this process before they actually died.)

Dream stages

Immediately after the loss, you may not remember any dreams for a while. After some time has passed, your dreams may contain feelings of foreboding or anxiety, but no specific cause for it. Your loved one

may or may not appear in the dreams. You often won't dream of the death itself until months later; it takes that long to understand, throughout the psyche, that the loss really happened. About six months after the death, you may have dreams in which your loved one is dead, and you increasingly come to realize in the dreams that they are really gone. Around this time, you may dream of the lost person, whom you now know in the dream is dead whereas you are alive. Sometimes your loved one just appears and does not communicate with you, but you are left with a feeling of peace or comfort. Other times,

you speak to your loved one and they may answer you or speak to you. These dreams can also give the feeling of being unable to reach the dead person (as in a dream where you shout to them from a distance, and are unheard), or vice versa. Don't be alarmed if you attack or yell in anger at your loved one. Anger is a stage of grief (see page 160), and its expression shows you are healing from the loss.

Healing dreams

In several instances, my clients had interactions with their loved ones in which the deceased asked if there was anything the dreamer needed. These dreams occurred even when the relationship between the deceased and the dreamer was strained in life, and helped dreamers not only to cope with the death, but with the realization that no healing with the person will ever take place in the outside world.

Lost children

Parents who have lost their children often have extremely painful dreams of the death, and then, as they begin to heal, dream of their children being in danger when they were younger. It is as if the parent's psyche recognizes something terrible has befallen the child and is trying to give the parent a chance to prevent it by presenting the child as younger in the dream—before the loss occurred. These dreams eventually blend with the knowledge that the child is now gone; parents will dream, for example, of their child when they were toddlers, only in the dream, they are dead. This happens even if the child died as a young adult. In this way, parents seem to be becoming aware that the child, present and past, has gone forever. I've seen these dreams followed, years later, by dreams in which the parent and the child have healing interactions that leave the parent feeling more at peace about the death.

Stages of Dreaming After a Death

In working with people grieving the loss of a loved one, I've found they often dream of their departed one in stages.

You may not remember any dreams at first, which seems to be a common initial response to any trauma. When you begin to recall dreams, they may be anxious dreams, without any overt cause. Over several months, you may begin to dream of your loved one as if she or he were alive. After about six months, a dream of the person, alive in the dream, may startle you, because you realize as you are dreaming, that the person is dead. These dreams can be very healing, as they often evoke calm, peaceful, loving feelings.

Is it true that you can't dream of something you haven't experienced... so if you die in a dream, will you die in real life?

Of course you will die in real life . . . eventually! Dreaming of death is one of the great, scary myths about dreaming. People dream of things they haven't experienced all the time. Some of us make up entirely new worlds in our dreams—seeing aliens, human machines, and all sorts of things that don't exist in the real world. You are at your most creative when dreaming because you are forced to conjure up every detail and interaction at lightning speed.

An urban legend

Accounts of people who dream of their own death and then die in the way they dreamed about are extremely rare. In general, dreams about dying tend to represent a passage from the old self to the new self (see page 161). Dreams about death tend to come before dreams of birth and babies (see page 100).

If these dreams aren't positive, they may be warning you that the way in which you are living in the world, and/or treating yourself, is harmful. If this is the case, then you should take notice of the warning that your dreams are giving you and examine how well you are looking after yourself.

What does it mean if I have the same dream over and over again?

Between one half and two-thirds of adults have had at least one dream that has repeated itself over time, and this is known as a *recurrent* dream. Most people have the initial dream in childhood which then becomes a recurrent dream. They are usually anxious dreams, but one study found that if they first occur later in life, recurrent dreams tend to be pleasant.

Important signals

Although Freud had little interest in recurrent dreams, Jung saw them as among the most important of all of our dreams. They show us that some inner, emotional conflict has not yet been resolved. Recurrent dreams show us the same issue again and again, reminding us that it is still awaiting resolution. Psychotherapists find that if you are willing to consciously tackle the problem that the recurring dream illustrates, your dream will change, and eventually end. Because recurrent dreams portray such important, central issues in one's emotional life, their resolution signals that a personality change has probably occurred.

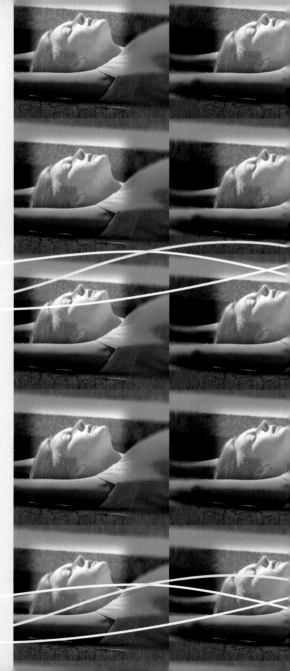

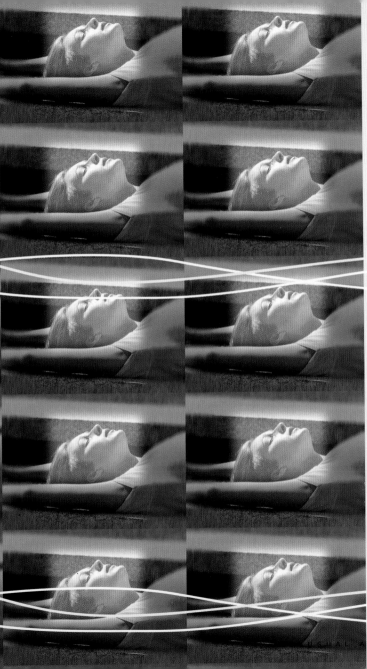

Recurring dreams and well-being

What kind of people would you expect to feel a greater sense of well-being: people who are having recurrent dreams; people who used to have them, but now no longer do; or people who have never had them? A study investigating that question found that past recurrent dreamers (those who no longer have them) feel better than either of the other two groups, and their dreams are also happier. The investigators explained this finding by pointing to the benefits of working through long-standing emotional problems that are then represented in later, more pleasant dreams.

What does it mean if you are dreaming and know you are dreaming?

This experience is called *lucid dreaming*, meaning that you become aware that you are dreaming while you are actually dreaming. Lucid dreaming was described by Saint Augustine over 1,500 years ago. The practice was also encouraged by Tibetan Buddhists in the eighth century, when it was used to help monks question the nature of consciousness and reality. It only became a popular topic for researchers over the past few decades, after two British investigators connected themselves to REM monitoring equipment and were able to signal with eye movements the point at which they became aware they were dreaming. A debate was then launched in the sleep research community as to whether lucid dreaming was real. That is, are people who do it actually asleep? It seems they are.

Lucid dreamers tend to have certain kinds of qualities. For some reason, people with good balance tend to have more lucid dreams than others (gymnasts have five times more lucid dreams than the rest of us). Lucid dreamers also have vivid imaginations and are easily able to become absorbed in inner experiences—one study found that those who like to read fantasy novels have more lucid dreams.

What are some techniques for having lucid dreams?

Stephen LaBerge, a well-known researcher, claimed that not only are some people able to become aware that they are dreaming, but those who've never experienced lucid dreams can be taught. He developed a "dream light" that is activated when dreamers enter REM sleep and acts as a cue to help them remember what they are dreaming.

Are you dreaming now?

There are several techniques that you can use to become aware you are dreaming. LaBerge has described various techniques for being able to tell whether or not you are dreaming. One of the most powerful ones is, in the dream, to look at something and then look away. Look back, and if the object has changed, you are dreaming. I have tried his suggestion myself...it took a few nights before I became lucid in a dream. I looked at a picture on the dream wall, looked away, looked back, and it was the same! Since then, I've never been completely sure whether or not I'm dreaming.

Use any of the techniques described in the panel opposite. Experiment with them and learn what works best for you, as practicing these techniques does increase your ability to become lucid in your dreams.

Aids to Lucid Dreaming

• Read about and talk to others about lucid dreaming during the day.

• Develop a ritual just before sleep with the intention of increasing your lucid dreaming: pray, meditate, stretch, or do yoga for example.

• Practice deep relaxation (see page 71) before you go to sleep.

• Tell yourself several times a day, and just before you fall asleep, that you will have a lucid dream.

• During your daily activities, continually ask yourself, "Am I dreaming?" Be sure to do so whenever your daily life feels dream-like.

• As Don Juan told Carlos Castaneda, look at your own hands while dreaming to trigger a lucid dream. Anything will do, for example looking at a particular object or saying a particular phrase. If you do this during your waking life, too, it will help you to remember to do it while dreaming.

• Decide to perform a particular action while dreaming, something you are unlikely to do while awake. Flying is a good choice, since many people spontaneously become lucid when they are flying in dreams. Remind yourself of your intention just before you fall asleep.

• Imagine yourself in a prior dream, but lucid.

• Get lots of sleep, since lucid dreams usually occur after several hours of sleeping.

• Wake up and then go back to sleep. One study showed that taking a nap after two hours of wakefulness produces three times as many lucid dreams as during a normal night of sleep. (Two hours seems to be the most productive period of time for being awake.)

• As you fall asleep, instead of counting sheep, just count, saying "I'm dreaming" after every number. ("1—I'm dreaming; 2—I'm dreaming . . .")

A friend of mine knows he is dreaming and can actually bring in characters and scenarios and then change the outcome of his dream. What are the advantages of this, and how can I learn to do it?

This practice is called *dream control*. It is distinct from lucid dreaming (that is, you can become lucid without doing anything to your dream) but obviously, being aware you are dreaming is a prerequisite for influencing it. There are positive and negative aspects to controlling your dreams (see the box on page 177). Dream control is really just another form of imagination—it just feels more real than a daydream would. Once you become lucid in a dream, the next step is simply to will the object or person you wish to see to appear, and then you can interact with your dream. It's as simple as that!

Advantages of dream control

People learn to control their dreams for several reasons. First, you may just want to have fun. Being able to fly in your dreams at will is exhilarating. Second, you may want to develop your creativity, or try to heal a physical problem. Third, dream control is sometimes used in psychotherapy to help clients

who are plagued by nightmares and shadow figures.

Fun is probably the most common use of the skill of dream control. Those who begin to practice it usually spend their first dream control experiences simply enjoying their dreams. They fly, they have sex with a lovely stranger or unrequited love, and they meet people they've always wanted to meet (or, at least, their own creations of those people).

However, expert dream controllers warn that the exhilaration fades. The awareness remains, but it no longer feels as it once did, and sometimes it can be unpleasant. Experts warn that you should focus on learning how to control your responses to >

events in your dreams (and life), not to creating the events (which shows disrespect for the unconscious).

Dream control may also be helpful for those who are seeking inspiration or the experience of being adept at new modes of creative expression. A young client of mine was a ballet dancer and having particular difficulty learning to tap dance. One night, she spontaneously realized she was dreaming and began to execute a complex tap routine. This experience gave her the confidence to continue on with her tap lessons, and also the sense of joy possible in that form of dance.

There are many anecdotal reports of people becoming healed after becoming lucid in dreams and then directing light to a diseased part of the body, or imagining it as beautiful and healed. The usefulness of this kind of dreaming, though, needs to be more fully studied.

Hazards of an overcontrolled dream life

Once you have changed your dream, you have imposed your conscious mind on it. In my book, *The Creative Dreamer,* I wrote that dreams are the one place we have left where we have no conscious control over what happens.

As the world becomes more and more uncertain, we naturally feel the need to control more and more. No wonder dream control has become so popular. Needing to control life can put our world out of balance, and lacks faith and respect for the wisdom and rhythm of nature and other people. It is also unrealistic: we are only human, just a small part of the universe, trying to fit in with each other and the natural world. None of us is God. I believe it's important for us to have a little reminder of that every night.

Pros and Cons of Dream Control

Pros: fun; relief from waking life stress; may give a sense of control to people who feel powerless in their waking lives or who are struggling with anxiety; may provide creative inspiration; may facilitate problem-solving.

Cons: unsuitable for people who do not have a strong hold on reality, or for people with mood disorders; danger of addiction; danger of substituting in fantasy what one needs to do in reality; control can be used as a defense to avoid the psychological substance of our dreams, to turn the nasty into the sweet; control can interfere with the healing attributes of regular dreams.

Use the descriptions in this part of the book to help you understand your dream language. Remember, no one can tell you with certainty what your own dreams mean. If you have been keeping a dream journal, read through it, identifying puzzling dreams or images. Otherwise, try to recall dreams that you have had recently, or found particularly vivid or intriguing. Refer back to the descriptions of dream theories and interpretation techniques throughout Part One to enrich the dreams you have to

Dream Directory

work with. Write down each striking image. Make notes on each image, and what each makes you think of, then look through the Dream Directory for the relevant entry.

The meanings of elements in the Dream Directory are gathered from history and from cultures around the world to help inform you about your own dream world. Gently attend to your own intuition, feelings, and quiet inner thoughts while reading. There are many possible meanings for every dream image. A bibliography at the end of the book suggests further reading that can help you explore in more depth.

The Natural Environment

THE SETTING IN WHICH you find yourself in your dreams can tell you a lot about your inner state. In my first book, *The Creative Dreamer*, I wrote about inner nature and the way in which dream settings tend to mirror the condition of our psyches. If you dream of a landscape in some kind of turmoil, that may reflect your feeling of upheaval on the inside. If the dream landscape is peaceful and placid, so much the better, as you are likely to feel calm, with inner chaos far away. The weather, temperature, and water as they influence your dreams, can similarly indicate your emotional state

Individual elements from nature that are shown here can provide a backdrop and emotional tone for lots of different dream themes.

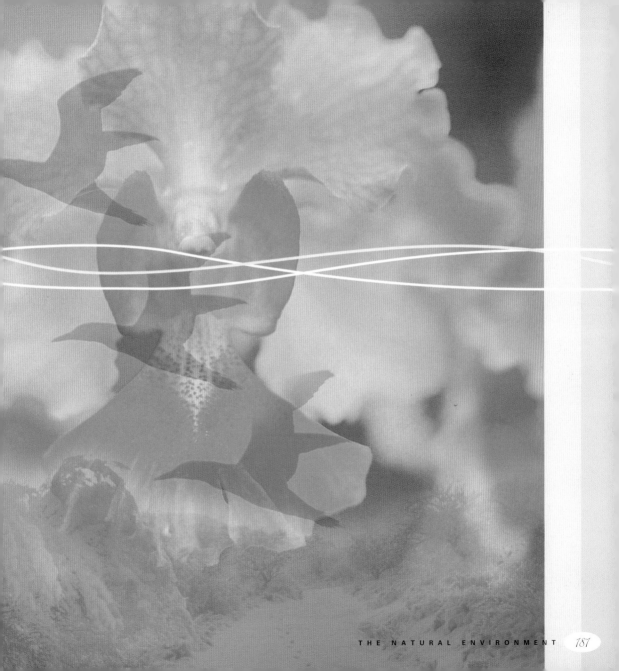

Weather Patterns

If climate plays a part in your dreams, it is typically just another element of the overall setting. However, weather is always important, as it sets the feeling and tone of the dream and can indicate your emotional and spiritual condition. In literature and film, weather is also often used as a metaphor. When sung, the phrase "stormy weather" evokes moodiness, for example.

Sometimes, though, weather will play a central role in defining the dream's action. For example, "I was at the beach and a tidal wave was coming . . ." At the time of these dreams, your feelings are often intense. Pay attention to dreams in which weather plays a part—they are likely to paint a clear picture of your emotional state. If you have many stormy dreams, remember, "feelings change with the weather"! Weather patterns in dreams tend to reflect current mood rather than long-term trends.

Storms

It was a dark and stormy night . . . Used as a metaphor in bad novels, and even by Snoopy of the *Peanuts* comic strip, this phrase conjures up a sense of foreboding. Storms suggest trouble on the horizon: our inner calm is threatened by approaching turmoil. In the religious art of many cultures, storms are used to illustrate change over time, and in India, storms represent the unlocking of creative energy.

Storm at sea

A storm at sea combines the symbolism of storms with that of the ocean and suggests the dreamer is experiencing a difficult inner conflict.

Storm at night

If you find yourself in a storm at night, consider how aware you are of troubles you may be experiencing. Are you "in the dark" about the problem? Is there a way to shed some more light on it?

Thunder and lightning

In China it was believed that when a dragon moved it produced thunder. In many religions, however, thunder signifies the voice of a deity, who is revealed through a flash of lightning. In ancient Greece, for example, thunder (associated with the god, Zeus) was considered to foretell the destiny of the country. However, divine power can be either destructive or life-giving. In the Bible, lightning occurs when God is angry, and thunder is His voice. Zeus, the ancient Greek god, was thought to hurl lightning bolts when he was annoyed.

In modern dreams, though, thunder and lightning often represent sudden, striking

intuition about a situation that illuminates the unconscious. We have just become aware of something about ourselves we did not know before.

Rain

Rain represents fertility in the art of most cultures, especially Asian. We all depend upon rain for water: in dreams, it is the life-giving, nourishing substance that revitalizes and purifies us. The rain is seen to come from the heavens, so in many ancient cultures it was a symbol for uniting earth and heaven, or our base nature with our spiritual one.

The following categories may also have resonance:

*O*cean
PAGE 200

*H*eat and Cold
PAGE 196

Winds

Of the four elements—earth, air, fire and water—air is considered by most peoples the most important, as it relates to breath. This is true, too, of wind. Through winds we sense air.

The people of Persia (ancient Iran) believed the wind mediated between the cosmos and earth, its purpose being to guarantee harmony and to support the entire world. Islam, Native American spirituality, and the ancient Chinese hold that the wind carries divine wisdom—the Chinese designated eight kinds of wind and used them for divination. The ancient Egyptians and Mexicans, though, considered wind to be a harbinger of evil, and this belief found its way into our modern saying, "an ill wind blows no good." Other traits of the wind are that it cannot be seen and easily changes direction. We speak of those aspects when we use such phrases as "she changes like the wind."

Wind features prominently in many plays, films, and books, from *The Tempest* to *Mary Poppins* and *Chocolat*. In these, wind signals a change is coming. If you dream of the wind, then, consider whether it may represent something passing away or coming to be, your spirituality, or a larger change in your life.

A gentle breeze

A gentle breeze indicates a less drastic change than would a blustery day. Change is in the wind, but you are not disturbed by it. You might even find it rather nice.

A fierce, howling wind

If you dream of a fierce, howling wind, the change or transition may be so major as to scare you. Notice your feelings in the dream. Are you afraid? Or exhilarated? If winds represent feelings for you, a strong wind deserves special notice. Your response to it in the dream may tell you more about how you cope with change: do you welcome it? Resist it? Barely notice it?

Wind outside, you inside

When the wind is outside, with you inside, you may have a bit more emotional protection from the change: you are observing it from a safe place, watching it, and will be better able to respond to it with the knowledge you are gaining.

Hurricanes or tornadoes

These are the extreme wind dream elements. Hurricanes combine water and wind (unconscious change or spirituality), whereas tornadoes are solely about wind (spirit).

The following categories may also have resonance:

*H*eat and Cold
PAGE 196

*T*he Heavens
PAGE 188

Q&*A* on end of the world dreams
PAGE 158

Sometimes alterations inside or outside of us are so complete they result in the destruction of what once was, so that something new can flower there. Such was the symbolism in *The Wizard of Oz*, where the dream tornado led Dorothy to a confrontation with the unconscious and the resulting development of the self.

Clouds

Anthropologists who studied cloud images in various cultures discovered that they usually represent spirituality. In the Judeo-Christian tradition, even in the Old Testament of the Bible, clouds signal the arrival of an important message from God, or represent an actual prophet. A fourteenth-century, anonymous English mystic's book, *The Cloud of Unknowing*, instructs initiates in going into the "inner clouds of the mind" for spiritual transformation.

In Greek mythology, clouds are where the gods actually live, and clouds and mist surround sacred mountains, obscuring them as the elusive, diaphanous boundary between heaven and earth. In James Hilton's classic novel, *Lost Horizon*, the hero describes his approach to Shangri-La, an otherworldly paradise:

"All afternoon the plane had soared through the thin mists of the upper atmosphere, far too high to give clear sight of what lay beneath. Sometimes, at longish intervals, the veil was torn for a moment, to display the jagged outline of a peak, or the glint of some unknown stream . . . far away, at the very limit of distance, lay range upon range of snow peaks, festooned with glaciers, and floating, in appearance, upon vast levels of cloud."

For the Chinese artist, clouds signal transformation. The *I Ching*, a Chinese method of divination used for over 3,000 years, describes 64 archetypal situations in which we find ourselves in daily life, and gives advice on how to navigate them from a spiritual perspective. According to the *I Ching*, clouds may signal the need for restraint in an unfulfilling or difficult situation.

What all of these perspectives have in common is that they view clouds as connected somehow with one's spirituality. If you've had a dream in which clouds appear, you might then consider whether it speaks to your spiritual life. Does your spiritual self need attention? Is it being obscured or hidden? Do you need to seek out your own inner wisdom, explore your religious feelings with more commitment, or seek out a new form of worship or meditation?

If you don't feel the above is apt, try asking yourself if your dream clouds might be an internal weather report. After all, a cloudy day obscures the sun and can "dampen one's spirits," whereas the sun breaking through the clouds makes us optimistic. Then, when asked during the day how you're feeling, you can reply truthfully, "mostly sunny, with a few clouds." You'll be surprised how many people will understand what you're talking about!

Sunny day with few clouds

A sunny day with few clouds is the image of the sky with which most fairy tales and childhood stories begin. All is well—although not perfect— and one's mood is generally bright and clear.

Thick mist or fog

Are you wandering in a dense mist or fog? What in the dream is being hidden by its veiled atmosphere? Consider whether something feels confusing in your daily life, and how the other elements of the dream might give you insight into what you are having difficulty "seeing" when you are awake.

A cloudy day

Such days suggests a dysphoric or uneasy mood, a slight feeling of the "blues," which might be caused by difficulty in a current situation obscuring the light of the sun. Don't be too concerned, as difficulties often precede clarity and renewed energy.

Dark clouds are approaching

If you see them coming, then take care! The unconscious may be reporting that you are

becoming aware of a conflict. Trouble may be on the horizon and tension may be building. Is there a situation in your life needing immediate attention, feelings or action.

>

The following categories may also have resonance:

Thunderclouds

Thunderclouds might indicate that trouble is just about to break. Perhaps thunder is beginning to rumble; the first sounds of conflict about an issue are manifesting in your life or conscious mind.

Looking down on clouds

When you are looking down on clouds while flying or from a high peak, you may be demonstrating, in the landscape of the dream world, your greater perspective on an issue. You can see what's been obscuring you, and you are now "above" it.

The heavens

For most peoples throughout history, the sky represents the active, masculine, spiritual principle. When we notice the sky in a dream, we tend to name something in it—plants, planes, birds, and so on. In that case, the sky becomes a stage backdrop, without much singular importance. But when the sky itself is described, this section may aid you in understanding its meaning.

The sun

In Islam, Hinduism, ancient Greece, Iran, India, and Egypt, the sun is the eye of the divine, of creative power. It is no wonder so many of us sometimes refer to the skies as "the heavens." The sun in the artwork of many cultures represents the hero, who is linked with the divine.

Jung writes of the sun as a symbol in dreams of the source of life, and of wholeness—a symbol of the self. Freudians interpret the sun as equivalent to fire, that is, libido, or life energy. The sun casts its light on all things equally, and is sometimes a symbol of justice and knowledge.

Sunrise, sunset

For Native Americans, the sun setting or rising symbolizes the cycle of life, from birth through death and rebirth. In art, the setting sun often represents the end of an age or, more literally, death. How high is your dream sun in the sky?

We also use sunrise and sunset as metaphors for beginnings and endings more generally. A beautiful dream sunrise or sunset suggests you are able to appreciate what is coming into or leaving your life or psyche.

Black sun

The image of the black sun is used in India to represent melancholy, death, or disaster. In dreams, it may illustrate something coming to an end and initiating a new beginning, a new rising sun.

Clear, blue skies

In a dream these are a positive backdrop for the dream action. They indicate that the dreamer's ability to discriminate, analyse, interpret, and to be objective (each of which are qualities of the archetypal masculine within us all) is unobstructed. "Clear skies ahead" is a phrase we use in our waking lives, too, to suggest that no disturbing weather patterns are "clouding" our judgment or putting us in peril.

Starless sky at night

When dreamers mention the night sky, they often say something like "it was so dark, it was black." In such dreams, we are in a sort of void. When you have a dream of a night sky without light, notice your feelings. Some psychologists interpret such a dream to indicate our experience in the womb, or feelings of safety or terror in the face of our existential aloneness in the world. Darkness in dreams often represents the unconscious. Whatever appears in your dark dream may illuminate your unknown "dark" psyche.

The following categories may also have resonance:

Clouds
PAGE 186

Storms
PAGE 182

Dream landscapes

The landscape reveals the foundation, or structure, of many dream settings. What are the elements in your dream landscape? What might they imply about your inner life? Is your psyche full of mountains or molehills? Do you have deep valleys, or wide, fertile plains? What is the state of your inner garden?

Many people dream again and again about a landscape they have never seen in waking life. These dreams are precious, because they are the result of your pure imagination—creating something from nothing, or knitting together pieces of places you've seen to make a new world which is more you than there!

Mountains and hills

In the mythology of many countries around the world, mountains and hills represent spiritual elevation, transcendance, and communication with the divine. These qualities are achieved by overcoming difficulty (the dangerous climb). Mountains lift our eyes upward and are closer to the heavens, so in many religions, places of worship are built on hills and mountaintops.

Mountains figure prominently in Western religion—think of Moses receiving the Ten Commandments on Mount Sinai and Christ on the hill at Calvary. In the English language, mountains are used metaphorically to describe challenging obstacles ahead, with their size being equivalent to the amount of difficulty. In this way, they symbolize our immutable, highest aspirations.

Looking up a mountain

If you dream you are looking up a mountain, then you might be gaining an objective view of your own spiritual condition, or of how large an obstacle you may be facing and how far you must travel in order to reach the "summit."

Looking down from the summit of a mountain

This suggests you have overcome an obstacle, and have a wide view of (or more perspective on) just how far you've come and where you've been. You must now go down the other side, though, which requires care and patience.

The inside of a mountain

If you're inside a mountain you are where the dead reside, according to the Celts. Mountains were also believed to house the magical faerie realm.

Mountain in an avalanche

Being caught in a mountain avalanche suggests that in trying to surmount an obstacle, you might be experiencing a sudden, threatening rush of feeling that was previously denied.

The following categories may also have resonance:

The heavens
PAGE 188

Heat and cold
PAGE 196

Gardens

As a place where nature is contained and ordered in response to our whims, the garden (versus the woods or sea) represents consciousness—specifically, the imposing of consciousness on the unconscious. In the Bible, the garden image implies innocence and primal temptation, with the Garden of Eden a symbol of Paradise. Hindu mythology also contains a paradisical garden at the center of the universe; gardens made by Hindus were grown in imitation of this most sacred space. In Japan, heavenly gardens rest in front of temples, synthesizing the universe with the sacred tree of life.

Gardens are also seen as refuges from the outer world. Jung wrote of gardens as the archetypal image of happiness, of the innocence of the soul. They are a place of growth, fertility, and germination of feelings and inner development.

Formal garden

A formal garden with a fountain in the center is the image of the Garden of Paradise in Islam. For Jungians, this image stands for the self.

Wild gardens

Wild gardens suggest free, unbridled life energy. If the garden is untended, perhaps you need to pay more attention to your more primal nature and needs.

Walled gardens

Walled gardens represent female sexuality in art and literature (e.g., *The Secret Garden*). Notice the integrity of the boundaries. Are they safe and strong, or are they falling apart? The walls around a garden may symbolize how protected and safe you feel your sexuality is from guests or intruders.

Kitchen or vegetable gardens

These suggest self-care and nourishment. How healthy and vibrant is your garden, or are there too many "bugs" inside? Is your inner garden in need of fertilizing?

Famous gardens

Famous gardens evoke the idea of collective, societal efforts to tame the wilderness, imposing order on chaos, for good or ill. They, like famous people, can represent the persona—our social role.

Valleys

Valleys signal life and abundance. They are fertile places where crops grow and new life arises; for Freudians, the valley represents the womb. In myths and fairy tales, shepherds and priests live in valleys, often in idyllic surroundings. As the opposite of the mountain, the valley also symbolizes depth. Some myths ascribe to valleys death and loss themes, while others see them as symbolizing experience and knowledge. In Taoism, valleys (where rivers typically flow and often converge) represent openness and spiritual force.

Deep valley, lodged in a canyon

This image is a striking one. It amplifies the idea of descent, of going into things (and yourself) deeply. It is also a protected space. The idea of a valley in a canyon may mirror a situation in the psyche where two parts of the self (shown by the earth beyond the two canyon walls) do not yet meet. The valley is the space between them, which needs to be explored before the two sides of oneself can come together.

Wide, fertile valley

Such an image emphasizes the part of valley symbolism that refers to nourishment. This is a place where you are fed, and where what you need is provided for you.

Dry valley

The opposite of the fertile valley, suggesting a place where the self is not being cared for, and the waters of feeling and the unconscious are not flowing.

River bisecting a valley

Consider if this is an archetypal dream (see pages 12–15). One of the most common landscape motifs is this very scene. Psychologically, it symbolizes contained and directed unconscious feeling flowing freely through the psyche.

>

The following categories may also have resonance:

Famous people
PAGE 212

Water
PAGE 198

Cliffs

The symbolism of cliffs is rather obscure. In English, we speak of being on the edge of a cliff as a metaphor for being at the "end of our rope," or for meeting great peril. A cliff implies elevation, and sometimes when we have become too elevated in our self-concept, we will have a dream where we fear falling. It is as if the dream is advising us that we've gotten a little too high, a bit too "big for our britches," and it takes us down toward reality.

Going over a cliff

This may represent having missed or not prepared sufficiently for danger inherent in the reality of the current situation. It also suggests that one is about to take a big risk.

Climbing a cliff

Similar to climbing a mountain, climbing a cliff suggests being willing to face danger in order to ascend toward a difficult goal.

Cliffs above the sea

Here is a dream that combines earth and water imagery, with the cliffs of awareness rising above the sea of the unconscious. Will you climb, will you fall, or will you dive?

Beaches

Beaches derive their meaning from the twin symbols of water and the bridge between land and and see. When you are on a shoreline, you are in-between consciousness and the unconscious. What is the condition of your beach? What is the water like?

Tides

If you are aware of the tide, note its direction. If it is coming in, unconscious forces are influencing the current situation. If it is going out, conscious awareness is advancing.

Polluted beach

Sadly, polluted beaches are becoming a common image in modern times. They may represent the true state of our ecology, or of contamination of the psyche by self-destructive feelings and thoughts, and those of others we've internalized.

Lying on a beach, being at a beach resort, or playing on a beach

These all suggest comfort with the unconscious, and safety regarding current feelings.

Threat or fear on a beach

The threat could be from a person or even from something like a prehistoric creature, which often acts as a gatekeeper to the unconscious. It may seem terrifying, but perhaps it is just trying to protect you from your own depths. If, however, the threat is more ambiguous, or just a vague feeling, ask yourself how you're feeling about the unknown, in general.

The following categories may also have resonance:

Mountains and hills
PAGE 190

Oceans and seas
PAGE 200

Heat and Cold

Heat and cold in dreams speak to the vibrancy of your emotional and spiritual lives. In nature, the opposing elements of fire and ice illustrate temperature most strikingly. Fire evaporates water, and ice freezes it, so both of these are related to the symbolism of water. Some psychologists see physical temperature as standing for emotional warmth or coldness.

Fire

In Egyptian hieroglyphics, fire represents health and life, superiority and control, and spiritual energy. As the agent of change in alchemy, fire transforms and purifies. The way in which it melts and then blends different substances has also made it a metaphor for love and union.

The ancient Greeks initiated the practice of cremation from their belief that fire frees the soul, and the myth of the phoenix points to the role of fire in themes of rebirth "from the ashes." Perhaps because of the way fire is made (through friction creating sparks), fire also symbolizes sexuality and regeneration. Tantric Buddhists link fire with kundalini, the vital life force that rises from the base of the spine.

Fire also has destructive symbolism; in Christianity, Satan is the prince of eternal fire and therefore punishment.

Endangered by a wildfire?

For Freudians, such a dream might indicate that your sexual and aggressive impulses are out-of-control, and therefore may become self-destructive. Others see wildfires in dreams as being destructive in order to regenerate the psyche.

Building engulfed by fire

This is a terrifying dream for most people. However, it is also an image of purification in many cultures, leading to spiritual transformation.

Contained fire

Contained fires, such as in a fireplace or campfire, suggest your impulses are under control, and the life force is burning brightly. If food is being prepared, you may be using your impulses well: to nourish yourself appropriately.

Molten lava and volcanic eruptions

These images often represent the emotion of anger. If you have a volcano dream, consider whether or not you are about to explode from deep in your center. Alternatively, volcanoes erupting mimic the tension and great release we experience in creative expression and sexuality.

Dry lava field

Dry lava fields, such as those found in Hawaii and other parts of the world, suggest the eruption has already happened and you are surveying its effects.

Snow and ice

The pure whiteness of freshly fallen snow has made it a symbol of peace and also of sexual purity (i.e., "virgin snow"). Ice, on the other hand, may represent frozen feeling, and resistance to the unconscious.

Being caught in a snowstorm or blizzard

This dream experience suggests that there is danger from feelings you have not been expressing or acknowledging.

"It's snowing outside . . ."

If, in your dream, you are inside watching a snowstorm outside, be content in the knowledge that you feel safe from the coldness, which you may perceive as coming from outside of you (from others, or from a situation in the outer world).

Slippery ice

Dreaming of slippery ice might give you a reality check: it can be perilous to constrain your feelings or to refuse to feel them.

Falling through ice

This may reflect a common fear of exploring your older feelings and then being harmed by them.

The following categories may also have resonance:

Buildings
CHAPTER 8, PAGE 244

Water
PAGE 198

Water

Water occurs in 15 percent of all dreams. So what does water mean? Water is the one element that experts universally agree represents life, the feminine, and for psychologists, the unconscious—where our deepest, most unrecognized feelings reside. We will use over 260 million metaphors during our lives, mostly when describing our feelings, and many include water. The association between water and feeling has made its way into our language and into our dreams.

Streams and rivers

Rivers are described as paradoxical symbols. They evoke the feeling of time passing, along with subsequent loss, yet they also represent renewal and the course of life.

The ancient Greeks and Romans deified rivers, portraying them as old men or the masculine image of the local god. In some remote places in Italy, you can still find Roman statues of these river gods.

Crossing a river

In many myths, crossing a river represents overcoming an obstacle, which allows one to reach another part of the psyche, or another state of mind.

River flowing down a mountain

Judaism sees a river flowing down a mountain as representing a state of grace.

River flowing to the sea

A river flowing to the sea is
an image of returning to the
unconscious. In Buddhism
and Hinduism, it symbolizes
dissolving in Nirvana.

Four rivers

Four rivers are symbols in
Christian art of the four Biblical
gospels.

Lakes

Lakes bear an association to death,
magic, and the unconscious. The
Irish believe that the Land of the
Dead is at the bottom of lakes,
and fairy tales hold that faeries,
nymphs, and water sprites live in
a realm under the surface of the
lake. Egyptian hieroglyphs depict
an underground lake as expressing
the occult and all that is
mysterious. In more modern art,
the lake is sometimes envisioned
as the eye of the Earth.

Psychologically, the lake
image suggests that feminine,
unconscious feeling is being
successfully contained by one's
inner nature. If the scene lacks
danger and all seems peaceful,
lakes can be a positive source of
renewal and vitality in dreams.

Calm, mirror–like lake

A calm, mirror–like lake surface
evokes contemplation and
self-reflection.

Fishing on a lake

If you are fishing on a lake,
what are you hoping to bring
up to consciousness from your
own depths?

Figures by or in lakes

Dreams of figures by or in lakes
may be either positive or
negative anima representations
(see pages 14 and 137).

**The following categories may
also have resonance:**

Weather patterns
PAGE 182

Valleys
PAGE 193

Oceans and seas

As images are the language of the unconscious, it makes sense that dreams would present our strongest feelings to us with visions of large bodies of water. Consider dreams you have had of the ocean. Of all the images of water appearing in our dreams, the ocean is the one most commonly used as a metaphor in art and literature. In addition to representing unconscious feelings, the ocean represents birth and renewal, and also potential destruction. It inspires awe because of its great size, and fear at how small we find ourselves within it. When you explore your ocean dreams, make sure you notice the weather and how it influences the ocean, where you are in the ocean, and how safe or comfortable you feel. Ocean dreams can illustrate how you feel about your deepest self.

Stormy seas

Is your dream ocean stormy? Perhaps you are beset by strong, unpredictable, and threatening feelings. Were there waves, and were they manageable (you can cope with this problem or feeling), or did they threaten to overtake and overwhelm you? How you handle the waves in your dreams may demonstrate how strong your feelings are at the moment and how well you are coping with them.

Clear sailing

Is the ocean calm and lovely? At the time of the dream, you may feel exceptionally able to handle anything that comes your way, either from within or without. How clear is the water? Can you see into the depths of your own self? Are your feelings clear, or are they murky or contaminated?

Watching the tides

Are you actually in the water? Or are you standing on the shore, observing it from a distance? Your stance will give you information about how comfortable you feel with your own unconscious. Do you like it? Does it frighten you? Do you want to dive in? Or are you worried about creatures from the deep?

Tidal waves

You are standing on the shore and see a tidal wave in the distance. There is nowhere to go.

This is a typical dream of a person in crisis, where the dreamer fears his or her inner resources are not enough to cope with the demands of the situation. Sometimes crises are purely internal: you have just realized something about yourself that is overwhelming and "washes away" your old sense of yourself. How you reacted to the dream tidal wave, and what you did to protect yourself, can show you how you respond to overwhelming life situations, and might even provide clues as to how to proceed this time.

Above and below water

If you are in the water, are you in a vehicle of some kind, which suggests you are moving along, not stuck in your feelings? Are you swimming, diving deeply, or staying close to the surface (being more superficial)? If you are under the water, are you safe and exploring? If you are in danger of drowning, you may be "flooded" with too much unconscious feeling. Your dream's message may be that you need to surface for air before diving again, and next time, perhaps not go so deeply into your feelings. When feelings are strong and overwhelming, it is best to seek the guidance of a trusted friend, therapist, or spiritual adviser.

Creatures of the sea

Are there animals or creatures emerging from your dream ocean? When something appears, pay close attention as it may be an emerging aspect of your own, unknown self. Even if it looks dangerous at first, it might just be able to help you once you get to know it better. (See Part One for ways to interact with dream figures.)

People in the ocean

If you find yourself in an ocean dream and you are not alone, the people you are with can give you insight into undiscovered qualities within yourself. What is it about this person that you need within yourself? People often appear in ocean dreams as helpful guides, companions, or even as enemies. Remember that these are parts of you—you made them up!

The following categories may also have resonance:

Weather
PAGE 182

People
CHAPTER 6, PAGE 202

Underwater animals
PAGE 242

Creatures
PAGE 148

Storms
PAGE 182

Human Characters

IN THE HISTORY OF Dream Research (pages 10–21) we
saw that the Gestaltist view urges us to explore our dreams
by considering that all of the people in our dreams
represent aspects of ourselves we may or may not know
well, or even be able to acknowledge. Looked at in this
way, each person in your dreams reveals parts of your
personality. What they reflect back to you about yourself
may seem positive or negative. Remember, though, that
dreams often exaggerate qualities and experiences.

Think about what each character in your dream
might represent about you. Take a close, fearless look. If
you were to describe this character's personality, what
words would you use? Do you typically express or

minimize these qualities in your waking life? Do you need to do so in order to overcome a current difficulty? Sometimes this is easier to do with characters we don't know in real life. If you dream of a person you have lost, consider what qualities that character represents in you that you have stopped expressing or have grown out of—in other words, what has "died" within you? If you have characters in dreams who cannot or do not speak, they may well represent a new function of your personality that is in the process of development.

Beyond the personal meanings you may glean from taking a close look at your dream characters, they may hold more universal meanings, too. Human characters in dreams can indeed be archetypal (see pages 12–15), symbolizing those collective, human attributes we all fear or fail to find in ourselves or others, as well as those we express or to which we aspire. The shadow tends to appear in dreams as a creature or a person of the same sex as you, whereas the anima (feminine) and animus (masculine) image appears as your opposite gender, often in the form of a crowd.

People We Know

Real people we know who appear in our dreams bring messages to us about how we perceive and feel about them in waking life. Dreams also show us when we are confused about a person, or when we are unconsciously exploring possible similarities between one person and another.

People we know make up the most frequent category of human characters in dreams. For men, 45 percent of all people in dreams are familiar, whereas for women it's 58 percent. Your dreams will demonstrate, over time, what kinds of people you are most preoccupied with, because those individuals will appear in your dreams (as in your waking thoughts) again and again.

The following categories may also have resonance:

*A*nimas
PAGES 14, 137

*M*ain dream theories (Jung)
PAGE 12

Q&A on sexual dreams
PAGES 130, 134

Lovers

Dreams of lovers can be either the most enjoyable or worrying of all dreams.

Interacting with a lover

When you dream of your real-life spouse, lover, or romantic partner, consider whether or not the person in your dream behaves the way you know them to do in waking life. If similar, this is a straightforward representation of your conception of your loved one, who may be accompanying you in the dream in the same way they do in waking life: as a companion. If different, think about who in your life actually has behaved in this way. Then you can make lists of each character's qualities. This can help you to distinguish between your unconscious "template" for a lover (which you may be projecting onto your real-life love), and the real, other person.

Archetypal images may also inhabit our dream world, appearing as imaginary dream lovers in "big" dreams. Jungian analysts Marie Louise von Franz and Emma Jung explored the stages of anima and animus development in their many writings. These archetypes change form as the dreamer becomes more aware of the aspects of the self they represent within the psyche. The anima first appears as a pure seductress, a woman of physical charms and interests (Delilah). Next, she is the cultivated woman of intelligence (Cleopatra). The third stage of the anima is the spiritual, ethically virtuous woman (Joan of Arc), and the fourth is the wise old woman (Mother Teresa). For the animus, the first stage is the man of physical and sexual power (Samson). The second stage is the man of action and initiative (Indiana Jones). Next, the animus is the intellectual man of words (Winston Churchill). Finally, as with the anima, the animus evolves into the wise old man (Gandhi).

The evolution of these stages as they appear in images of men and women in dreams suggests that the dreamer is becoming aware of and integrating their feminine side (if more masculine in waking life), or masculine side (if more feminine). Our dream anima/animus representations tend to match where we are in our waking life. Notice how, as the stages progress, each one contains the qualities of the ones that have come before. The stages become more complex and less stereotypical, just as our perceptions of other people grow as we develop psychologically.

The people we are involved with in real life can also hold aspects of the anima or animus, so when real-life lovers appear in dreams, they may also be taken as an animus or anima figure. Consider what stage your dream lover represents, and see whether you can find qualities in him or her from the other stages, too.

Partner from the past
Ex-loves often appear in dreams, especially when you are just getting to know a new person, or when there is tension between you. In the beginning of a relationship, you're trying to learn who the new person is and to see clearly the differences between present and past loves. Your dreams of past partners can help bring back to you what it was actually like to be with the past person versus your current love.

Your lover turns into someone else
See Q&A on metamorphoses on page 142.

>

Social contacts

Your dreams are populated with the same people with whom you interact during the day. The way in which you portray people in your dreams whom you don't know well in waking life can suggest potential for these relationships. If you dream about an acquaintance as if they were closer to you, perhaps your dream self is picking up on some similarity between you that could make for a good friendship.

Friends

Of all the familiar people who appear in our dreams, about two-thirds are friends and acquaintances. Just as dreams highlight feelings and thoughts you may be having about loved ones, so they also depict emotions about people less close to you.

Dreams about friends and acquaintances also suggest your social life is what you think about most, and could give you a clue as to how supportive you find these individual relationships.

Work associates

If you are having a lot of dreams about work colleagues, you may be preoccupied with some problem with which your work is presenting you, or with work itself. Having more dreams about colleagues than about social contacts or family might also indicate your life is slightly out of balance. Work, itself, can also be a metaphor for inner work you are doing.

Family

You will dream of the family you grew up with throughout your life. Childhood family members appear consistently in the dreams of middle-aged and older adults, who also tend to repeatedly dream about the house or neighborhood in which they grew up.

You will also dream of people who do or have mattered to you, including the family you've created (spouse and children, or a close group of friends and community). The more attached you are to a person, the more likely it is that you have felt many different feelings for (and with) that person. They have touched you, and even surprised you. The deeper your emotions for someone, the more vulnerable you are to the potential loss of them, and, paradoxically, the more joy and peace you are capable of feeling in their presence. Our emotional memory links the deep feelings of attachment we have right now for the people in our present life with those feelings we have had in the past for people who may be gone. This is done unconsciously and so we are mostly unaware of it. But whatever pain or joy we experienced with people we were once attached to, these feelings are often expected now with new people.

Some schools of psychology hold that all of our conceptions of people in adulthood are rooted in and colored by our very first relationships with our family. Most psychologists believe that at least some of our expectations of others originated in childhood, as we learned a template or pattern for how relationships work. This pattern was "grooved" into our psyche, and it is very difficult to change. If, for example, your family were not physically affectionate with one another and instead frequently bought each other presents, your template might contain the idea, "If I love someone, we don't touch much, but gift-giving is important." If you mate with someone who has the opposite template, then problems will arise (due to a mismatch of your templates), and these can only be solved through clear communication of your wants and needs.

Exploring the way in which your family members appear in your dreams, how they interact with one another and with you, can help shed light on exactly what you learned about relationships early on. Then you can examine your present relationships to see if these early "rules" are operating. Once you've done that, you can decide whether or not you feel it is useful or desirable to continue believing what you learned in the past. You can also talk with your loved ones about your expectations to clear up any misunderstandings that arise.

About one-fifth of all the known characters in your dreams will be family members. As with other people in dreams, family members can represent themselves (that is, your conceptions of them), and also parts of your own psyche. This is especially true in archetypal dreams, as we discover on pages 208–211.

>

Child

Sometimes a dream child will represent you as you were in childhood, and may give you information about what you needed in your early years, what interested you then that you might want to explore now, and how current sensations might be invoking feelings from the past.

The archetype of the eternal child is called the *Puer Auternus* (masculine) or *Puella Auternus* (feminine). Children in archetypal dreams may symbolize a new part of the psyche or the qualities of innocence, openness, creativity, irresponsibility, and renewal. This theme has been explored by several leading authorities.

In-laws

Clients have often told me about dreams where their parents' personalities are contained within the bodies of their very different in-laws, as if the dream is hiding the dreamer's parents by making them look like their spouse's parents. In this way, the dreamer is one more step removed from the way in which he or she portrayed them in the dream. Not surprisingly, this seems to happen most frequently in dreams that portray the in-laws negatively. In-laws can also be shadow figures of the parental images within us. We all carry echoes of our parents' voices within us, who let us know what we "should" and "should not" do, and sometimes these echoes appear as in-law characters in our dreams. Psychoanalysts see parental figures as representing the superego, that part of the mind we call our conscience.

Mother

The Great Mother archetype appears in different guises in dreams—as a nurturing figure, or in her negative aspect, as a devouring or raging monster. The latter portrayal can be quite terrifying, echoing feelings small children have when their very large mothers become angry. The way in which your dream mother nurtures you (or doesn't) can also give you a clue as to how well you are mothering yourself. Seeing the mother figure in your dream as a picture of the part of yourself responsible for taking care of you can be a vivid and enlightening experience. Does she need to be kinder to you? Is she expressing, in the dream, a legitimate concern about something you need to attend to in your daily life?

Father

Archetypal fathers teach their children how to be safe in the world, and how to act in order to succeed. Dream fathers also fulfill these functions. When you dream of a father figure, ask yourself whether or not you feel safe, whether you need to attend to your physical well-being, or require guidance in order to achieve your goals in the outside world. Does the dream figure offer this? Can you use his guidance when you're awake? Is there anyone else you know (including your own father) who might be able to offer these qualities to you now? Do you need to develop them within yourself?

>

The following categories may also have resonance:

"Big" vs. "little" dreams
PAGE 13

Q&A on dreams of childhood
PAGES 100–104

Q&A on id-ego-superego
PAGE 144

Grandparents

In big dreams, grandparents may represent the archetype of the wise old man or woman. These figures offer guidance, often of a spiritual nature, as well as nurturance for your true self. Sometimes they act as guides, pointing the way to something you need.

If you receive a gift from such a dream character, pay close attention to it. In such cases, the unconscious is presenting you with important information. What have you unlocked? What has become clearer to you? Often, these gifts are metaphorical or utilize puns or double meanings. For example, one client I worked with was afraid that if she started her own business, she wouldn't be able to support herself financially. She dreamed that her grandparents, long passed away, were standing in a bank. Two men stood between the two elderly figures. (She knew the two men in real life, finding them irritating and somewhat invasive.) The old woman and man then joined hands, pushed over the two men, turned to the dreamer and handed her a small sack of money.

When she awoke, the dreamer was puzzled as to why her grandparents would knock over two men in order to get her some money. After we discussed it, she realized both men were named Bill, so her grandparents had joined together to overcome her bills! Although the dreamer was fiercely independent in her waking life, instead of launching out on her own, she decided to mimic the dream and accept the support of a partner, with whom she launched a successful business.

Had she wanted to, she could have also taken this dream as reflecting an inner need to join the masculine and feminine sides of herself together in order to achieve success in the outside world. There are multiple interpretations for any dream, but the important thing is to recognize the interpretation that feels most helpful to you.

Siblings and other relatives

Siblings in archetypal dreams frequently represent shadow figures who are very near to consciousness; so close that in the dream you're related. Pay attention to the way in which your dream siblings and other relatives behave and the qualities they exhibit. Then use the exercise on page 127 to explore these shadow qualities in yourself.

If your relative turns into someone else then see page 142, the Q&A on metamorphosis.

The following categories may also have resonance:

Q&A on **metamorphoses**
PAGE 142

Q&A on **meeting the shadow**
PAGE 127

People We Don't Know

People we don't know in dreams often express the archetype of the shadow. Like the anima and animus, the shadow appears in dreams in stages. These stages represent how conscious we are of those qualities within us that the shadow embodies. Initially, the shadow may appear in a dream as a creature or object with life-like qualities; next, we may dream of an animal. The shadow is then represented as a person we don't know. Sometimes, we finally dream of the shadow as someone we do know—siblings or even ourselves.

We often feel threatened by shadow characters (as we do by the qualities and energy they represent within us); sometimes we feel deeply admiring or in awe of them.

Famous people

Prominent characters are relatively rare in dreams (only about one percent of all people in dreams are famous), so you should pay close attention when they do appear. They suggest that you want to be admired and esteemed, or simply known and recognized by others.

Dreams of famous people tend to fall into three categories: seeing a famous person; meeting a famous person; and being friends with a famous person. All kinds of things can happen within each category, and each type of dream implies different things about the dreamer.

Seeing a famous person

When you dream you are watching him or her on stage or elsewhere, consider whether or not you are observing a part of yourself that might hold that particular talent—perhaps in a less exaggerated form. If you dream of Tony Blair, for example, perhaps you have a talent for public speaking. Having dreams of Cleopatra? It could be time to let your sexual power show.

Meeting a famous person

If you dream of meeting a famous person, you are often meeting that person's most outstanding qualities within yourself for the first time. How can you nurture these?

Being friends with a famous person

These dreams can be quite fun. You have been chosen by someone you imbued with admired, larger-than-life qualities, so by association you are reminded that you are also special. Prominent people can befriend you in dreams when you are feeling a bit ordinary and lost in the crowd. They can also provide inspiration and encouragement for your own soon-to-be-famous work.   >

The following category may also have resonance:

Q&A on dreams of movies, film, TV
PAGE 140

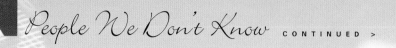

Artists and writers

The art of a people reflects their fears, desires, and values. Some artists and writers see themselves as translators for the human condition; others see themselves as channelers. Artists most often express themselves (and create feelings in the viewer) nonverbally, while writers use words. Both express undercurrents of feeling in society. When you dream of a famous artist or writer, ask yourself if there is something you need to communicate, perhaps something outside yourself.

Artists and writers also create something from nothing—fiction writers make up whole worlds. Are you, or can you, tap into your own creativity? Is there any way in which your view of a current situation could be unreal? Can you see your life as if it were a story being narrated, and if so, might this help you to step back from it to get a wider view? Journalists and non-fiction writers are supposed to record reality, so if you dream of them, ask yourself if you are paying attention to the facts of the situation that you are dealing with in waking life.

Entertainers

When you dream of an entertainer, think about his or her image. What do you believe they represent? What kind of person do they seem to be? How do they spend their time? Are these things you might want to do, or do already?

Dreams about famous entertainers abound. A fascinating book of dreams about the singer, Madonna, has been published, and Marilyn Monroe continues to appear in many people's dreams. Other entertainers who are frequent dream stars include Michael Jackson, various members of the Beatles, and a number of actors and actresses. Each of these individuals exists as a specific image. Some market that image on purpose; others have had the image evolve over time.

Often, dreams of entertainers include a moment when the dreamer realizes the entertainer is "just like me," or "just another person." When that happens, you may be exploring the difference between the persona and the real self. Are you your mask? Or are you what's beneath? Is it your unofficial job to entertain the people you know, or can you relax and just be yourself?

Politicians

Political figures can be good substitutes in dreams for your parents—that dream Congressman may act like your father, while Margaret Thatcher uses a phrase your mother often said. After all, politicians are powerful, control the "world" (as your parents did in your childhood), help pass laws, enforce order, punish, make proclamations, and so on.

What are your dream "politicians" like? Another way to explore the meaning of these characters is to view them as snapshots of your own ego functioning. (Of course, politicians can also be just . . . politicians.)

>

The following categories may also have resonance:

*A*rchetypes (persona)
PAGE 14

Q&A on ego
PAGE 144

Scientists

Scientists are quite rare in dreams, except in the dreams of scientists. If anything universal can be said about them, it would be that they represent the thinking function of the psyche. This function helps us to evaluate information based on facts, logic, and impersonal analysis (compared to the principles or values of the feeling function). When scientists appear, you may need to use more—or less—of this kind of decision-making. If your dream scientist is mad or out-of-control, you may be relying too much on logical thinking. Make sure your values and strongest principles are being considered, too. If your scientist is brilliant and competent (e.g., Einstein or Marie Curie), try observing your thinking function a little bit more and see what happens.

Sports heroes

Sports figures introduce such themes as competition, cooperation, achieving success through physical exertion and perseverance, and overcoming adversity by taking risks. Consider which of these themes might be active in your life at this time. Is there a lesson the sports figure might teach you about a difficulty you are facing right now? Is there something in the dream that might address your physical goals?

Philanthropists

Each term, undergraduates in a class I teach on community psychology tend to dream of people who are doing good works in the world, contributing their time or resources to help others. I see these dreams as illustrating a wish by the deepest self to give. These dreams revive us in times of cynicism about the world and can help motivate us to emulate those we admire through our own behavior.

Strangers

Dream strangers are those who, when you awaken, you do not know. If you are uncertain about someone's identity, you cannot really be sure this is a stranger. If you are like the average person, strangers account for 23 percent (for men) and 17 percent (for women) of all the characters in your dreams.

Even if you are dreaming of someone you don't know, someone who doesn't exist, someone you completely made up, you cannot really create someone from no one. You've had experiences with people all of your life. Whereas in the early 1800s most people in Europe and the U.S. saw a total of about 100 people during their entire lifetime, you now see that number or more every single day—if not in person, then in films and on television. You've met hundreds of people and know dozens well. Those you've spent the most time with have helped you decide how people are. Other experiences you've had or heard about and even news accounts you've seen inform you about what other people you don't know are like (or at least what they've done that has become newsworthy). All of the things you've learned about people find their way into your dreams. Strangers, though, show you most clearly what your perceptions of people in the world are likely to be, because a dream stranger (unlike a real-life stranger) is given qualities from inside your own mind.

Individual strangers

Jungians see an individual man or woman in a dream as representing parts of your psyche you are meeting for the first time. Often, they can be shadow figures.

Crowds

Crowds represent the animus (the masculine side of the psyche). They may also suggest that you are feeling isolated, impersonal, and unrelated in the world at the moment.

>

The following category may also have resonance:

*A*nimus, shadow, archetypes
PAGE 14

Lunatics

Crazy people are relatively common in dreams. Most of us have had fears of going mad at one time or another, so the dream lunatic presents us with a picture of pure irrationality that can, at times, be oddly soothing. Being rational all the time can be exhausting! In its most extreme form, the lunatic dream figure can represent a need to throw logic to the wind or may serve as a reminder that you are not crazy (otherwise, how would you recognize the lunatic?).

Guides

See grandparents.

Dangerous strangers

Murderers and rapists are so common in dreams that if we held to the idea that people dream about exactly what happens to them in real life, then we'd all be victims. People who have actually experienced horrifying physical and/or sexual violence will dream about those experiences long after they have happened. But for those of us who haven't been threatened in these ways, such dreams can be puzzling and alarming. When we awaken, we ask ourselves, where on earth did this dream come from? We may find ourselves locking our doors and windows and becoming a bit more frightened at night after such a dream.

Like all dreams, those of dangerous strangers are most often about ourselves. They can be taken as a sign that something within us is breaking into consciousness, or invading us intimately. Occasionally, this can be a self-destructive urge or impulse. If you frequently have these kinds of dream and are disturbed by them, you should seek the help of a spiritual adviser or psychotherapist.

Such dreams can also caution us to reinforce our *ego boundaries*. Boundaries tell us and others where they stop and where we begin. When your boundaries are firm, you have a clear sense of what is and what is not acceptable to you regarding how you are treated by others. Communicating those boundaries is called *limit setting*. When you dream of someone intruding on you, breaking into your house, accosting you verbally or physically, or raping you, you may need to examine the extent to which you feel emotionally invaded in real life. If this is true for you, you might consider how you deserve to be treated, what you will and will not tolerate from others, and then let others know.

Vocation

Dreams of people identified only by what they do for a living (9 percent of women's and 17 percent of men's dream characters) can be very telling. Such dreams capture and illustrate the persona, the mask we all wear to function in society. In a way, all vocational characters in dreams are actors: they show you the roles with which you are most familiar in your own life, and sometimes suggest new roles you might try to adopt.

Religious vocations

Religious guides such as a nun, priest, or monk suggest a theme of spiritual wisdom. They may appear when you feel a need to return to your spiritual values, re-examine your beliefs, or commit to a spiritual life.

Royalty

Princesses who star in fairy tales, and are often seen as victims, may symbolize undeveloped or stifled feminine qualities, while princes tend to be action-oriented heroes in many legends. Princesses tend to mature into more aware queens, a symbol of feminine power. The king, on the other hand, is the archetypal masculine, with clear consciousness, discrimination, and sound judgment. The king's particular personality type represents whatever part of one's psyche is in control at the moment. Dreaming of a weak king may suggest you need to express or experience more feminine qualities (nurturance, harmony, emotion, relationship). The old king, for Jungians, is a strong symbol of the wisdom of the collective unconscious. The king and queen together represent the joining of the conscious and unconscious. >

The following categories may also have resonance:

Q&A on dreams and trauma
PAGE 110

Q&A persona
PAGE 14

Criminals

In dreams, criminal figures represent the nefarious motives and impulses dreaded and feared by society. From a psychological point of view, dream criminals act out in their behavior the raw, instinctual, sexual and aggressive desires we are born with—without constraint.

Being in prison

This illustrates the feeling of being trapped within one's own unconscious pattern, and, by extension, within one's own waking life. If you dream of being in prison, consider whether some self-destructive behavior or self-defeating pattern of thinking may be active in your life.

Escaping from prison

This suggests you might be able to overcome these unconscious forces and become free of them.

Police and judges

Authority figures, in contrast to criminals, are the ego of society: they are responsible for identifying and containing the expression of instinctual desires. Watch the way these characters interact with the criminals in your dreams, and/or with you. Who is stronger? This can indicate the way in which your id, ego, and superego function with your psyche.

Farmers

Farmers cross-culturally symbolize regeneration and renewal, as well as the passage of time in seasons, which are metaphors for aging. Farmers also nurture seeds into plants, which die and reseed and grow again, suggesting spiritual transformation and rebirth are at work.

Teachers

When teachers appear in your dreams, they lend themselves to questioning. What are you learning, in a larger sense? Are you paying attention? Do you need the lesson? Are you the teacher? And of whom?

Accountant or banker

Some believe that, in the modern world, money symbolizes neglected feelings about one's inner value(s) and the worth of outer relationships. Psychoanalysts see one's attitude toward money as reflecting one's need for power or control. If these dream characters appear, check to see if they are miserly or generous. What is your "worth"?

Shopkeeper

What is being bought (brought into yourself) and what is being sold (offered to the outside world)? At what price, and with what attitude and style?

Mystical occupations

Rarely do we dream of wizards, crones, and sorcerers (often another manifestation of the wise old man or woman archetype). These are more often found in fairy tales, where they suggest that powerful, unconscious forces of creativity and transformation are operating.   >

The following category may also have resonance:

Q&A on id-ego-superego
PAGE 144

Doctors, nurses, surgeons

These professionals help to heal people; in that way, they are linked to the ancient vocations of the shaman, healer, and medicine man. In what way does healing need to be brought to your current situation? Does the dream suggest this is possible? What are the difficulties involved? Does something need to be "cut out," or removed, from your situation or your attitude toward it? What needs to be nurtured? These characters often appear early in dreams of psychotherapy clients as representing the therapist.

Postal workers

Mail workers are messengers. When you dream of a post office, mailperson, or letter, consider that the dream might be bringing you a message you need to heed.

Creative types

Creative people may dream more often of artists, writers, and so on. Dreaming of an artist when you are one may actually help you to get through a creative block, if you are willing to dialogue with the character as described in Part One. Otherwise, artists represent the creative side we all have within us. How is your artist faring? Is she or he "starving"? Are there conditions in the dream that nurture the artist which you could create in your waking life to nourish your creativity?

Psychologist or other psychotherapist

People in therapy often dream of their therapists, but many clients are embarrassed to tell their therapists about their dreams. Don't be!

Dreams of having your therapist appear while you are talking to your parents or are back in your childhood environment are extremely common. Dreams of your therapist behaving like a friend or in a frightening, untrustworthy way might reflect difficulty trusting your therapist, a wish to be like or be liked by them, or a real problem in the therapy. Such dreams are very important and normal; if you have one, do tell your therapist about it.

Tradespeople

Dreams of people in the trades, especially those who are involved in work on houses, tend to occur during times of change, when we are rebuilding or even "remodelling" ourselves. >

The following categories may also have resonance:

*B*uildings
CHAPTER 8, PAGE 244

Q&A on dreams as inspiration
PAGE 54

The Animal Kingdom

ANIMALS APPEAR IN SEVEN to 13 percent of Western adults' dreams, and approximately five percent of all adults' dream characters are animals. The most frequently appearing animals in dreams are dogs and horses, followed by cats, birds, and snakes. Children dream a lot about animals—over three times as often as adults do. Like adults, they dream most about dogs and horses, then, in descending order of frequency: cats, snakes, bears, lions, and . . . monsters!

In many different cultures, animals are deified or symbolize spiritual forces. These cultures use animals in storytelling to help community members learn how to negotiate life's passages and challenges. Shamanic societies believe that each individual has a **totem animal**, or **spirit**

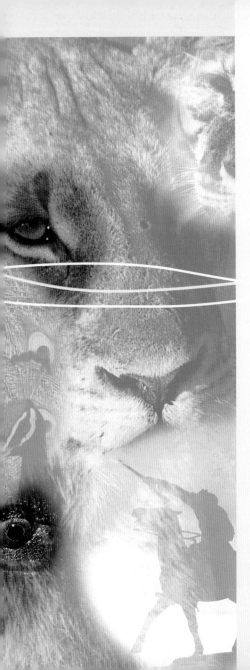

totem. This animal helps people to understand how the spiritual world is manifesting itself in their life, and animal totems often reveal themselves through a series of dreams. These spirit totems are considered to be a sort of alter ego, with the qualities and abilities that the individual needs to develop and honor. Therefore, for shamanic cultures, dreams in which animal figures appear are among the most important of all of our dreams.

Animals were also associated with the spirit world in ancient times, and rock paintings have shown the use of animals in religious rituals. Sacrifices of particularly healthy and strong animals were meant to appease the gods in many cultures, and to ensure fertility of the land and continued prosperity. Ancient societies took note of the natural world in order to make sense of what seemed to be the supernatural forces of the rain, sun, drought, and other weather conditions. Some cultures, including that of ancient Egypt, worshipped animal gods and goddesses.

\>

Modern psychologists see in animals symbols for unconscious, instinctual energy (or, in Freudian terms, the id. The more primitive the animal (see page 144), the deeper or more base the instincts it expresses. Fighting with—or taming—an animal, then, brings to mind the idea that you are working to manage your own instinctual desires. Having positive, friendly interactions with animals suggests that you are in harmony with your deepest longings and impulses.

Medieval animal symbolism, which found its way into fairy tales, depicts a typical story: the hero fights an animal, tames it, and is then served by it. The story of Saint George and the dragon and the tales of King Arthur and his knights teach us how instincts can be vanquished and used to serve our conscious purposes.

This theme is represented in the art of Persia (ancient Iran) and Assyria (Syria), where animals that are more highly developed triumph over those that are less so, symbolizing mastery over instincts. It is also echoed in the Native American and Mexican cultures, in the classic tale of the eagle's struggle with the snake. Relatively modern films and literature, including *Moby Dick* and even the *Jaws* series, seem to end at the point where the animal is vanquished, without being integrated and transformed into a helpful energy. Containing or taming one's instincts so completely that they cease to exist may lead to a disappointing, deadened life without feeling. Being unwilling to acknowledge that these powerful impulses reside within each of us can result in endlessly projecting them upon others in the real world, and then trying to destroy those others through war.

A fascinating series of studies found that animals in dreams do, indeed, seem to represent our unacceptable and "unbridled" instincts and impulses. Struggling with the beast within makes us anxious, which explains why animals in dreams usually make the dreamer feel apprehensive.

As you will see, almost every dream animal has a variety of meanings, depending upon the culture in which it lives. One way to use this chapter of the book is to first write down your own associations to the animal in your dream— your own memories pertaining to it, and your immediate reactions and feelings about it. Then, read through the descriptions here, seeking a feeling of "rightness" about one of them, or paying attention to where your thoughts lead you as you are reading.

Remember to look for something that might relate to an unacknowledged instinct, impulse, or hidden desire or fear. Then, consider the animal to hold a message from the unconscious. If you open yourself to becoming curious about it, you may find the animal transforming in subsequent dreams. But because your dream animal was created by you, only you can unlock its meaning. Here are some suggestions for where to begin.

Creepy Crawlies

There are over 800,000 insect species on Earth. In their multiplicity, insects are remarkably hardy and adaptable, and they are physically protected by a strong skeleton. Many scientists speculate that long after humans are extinct, insects will still make the Earth their home. Insects don't get tired easily, and are strong (bees, for example, can haul an object 300 times their own weight). Insects also have antennae, which allow them to sense danger (akin to human intuition), and to find nourishment easily. Finally, they physically change from one form to another. All of these qualities make insects very interesting dream symbols.

Although spiders do not actually belong to the insect species, they are included here for want of a more appropriate place.

Bees

Bees appear in the Bible, and in Imperial France, as symbols of royalty and wealth. In the art of ancient Rome and Greece, bees represented conscientious, diligent work; organized, communal life; and obedience to society. The Moslem, Egyptian, Delphic, and some South American traditions symbolize the souls of the departed as bees. Bees may also symbolize fertility.

A swarm of bees

Dreaming of a swarm, which feels dangerous to you, suggests you may feel threatened by what bees represent to you. If that is collectivity, you may be afraid of losing your individuality.

Bees in a hive

Bees in a hive are busy performing tasks to nurture the queen and the other members of the hive. If you dream of a hive, consider your relationship to work and to your family. In medieval Christian art, the beehive represented Mary, and the bee, Jesus Christ.

An individual bee

Dreaming of a single bee, away from its fellows, suggests individuality amidst society. As with dreaming of a swarm, if the bee seems dangerous to you, consider whether independence may be an issue in your life at present.

Caterpillars

We all know the tale of the caterpillar who believed, when it began to spin its cocoon, that it was dying, only to wake up a gorgeous butterfly. Caterpillars signify transformation, shedding the old to make way for the new; changing identity; or passing into another stage of life.

Caterpillar in a cocoon

As a metaphor for the self within the incubation stage of any transition, if you dream of caterpillars in cocoons, ask yourself how you may be pulling in from the world and preparing for a change.

Butterfly

Butterflies are associated with joy and completed transformations, coming out the other side of a perhaps difficult metamorphosis in your life, and therefore being free of the past.

>

Spiders

The most common creepy crawly to appear in dreams is the spider, which also appears in the mythology of all cultures. Spiders have a variety of connotations: they creatively weave an intricate and beautiful web; and they trap, encase, and devour their prey while sitting squarely in the center of the web. Spiders may, therefore, be a wonderful symbol of creativity (they make something useful where nothing existed before, using only themselves), or of the center. Native Americans see the spider as a grandmother (linking past and future) and creator. In India, spiders represent Maya, or the weaver of the web of illusion. Spiders continuously build and destroy, representing ongoing forces of change in life. From a Jungian perspective, the spider symbolizes the unhappiness associated with too much self-focus.

Black widow spiders

Black widows have, in their name and behavior, a clue to their symbolized meaning. They kill and eat their mates after sex, and, as such, they may represent the dark feminine side or the "devouring mother." They are, however, remarkably timid spiders, and a bite from one might make you sick, but will not kill you.

Tarantulas

They may appear in dreams representing the autonomic nervous system, as they bear a visual resemblance to the spinal column and vertebrae. Tarantulas do not weave a web, but rather spin a single thread upon which they somehow, in all their large size, manage to balance.

For their fearsome appearance, tarantulas are not dangerous to humans, and are actually extremely fragile: if you drop one, you will kill it.

Ants

Ants are quite successful evolutionary beings. They've long existed in their present form and thrived in their organized, collective life. Ants symbolize collectivity (as opposed to individuality) just as bees do. If you dream of ants, be sure your unconscious isn't using a pun—for "aunts"!

Cockroaches

Another successful ancient creature, cockroaches are interpreted by Freudians as representing male sexuality in dreams.

Land-based Mammals

Mammals appearing in dreams have a variety of meanings. Keep in mind, though, that animals often represent instincts and impulses. Note the way in which the particular mammal behaves and reacts to you or the dream action, as well as your feelings toward the animal while in the dream state. Your dream may illustrate the way in which your own psyche reacts to strong, unconscious impulses within you.

The following categories may also have resonance:

The animus
PAGE 14

Pets

Of all dream animals, about 20 percent are either domestic dogs or cats. Because we dream of those who populate our lives, this percentage is not surprising. If animals represent instincts, then domesticated ones may symbolize those impulses we have tamed.

Our pets also provide a calming, reassuring presence. One study found that anxious children tend to dream more often of domesticated pets, whereas less anxious children dream of undomesticated animals, such as deer and bears.

Cat

Cats, like snakes, are paradoxical symbols (in fact, Buddhism links the symbolism of snakes with that of cats). In some cultures (e.g., in Japan and medieval Europe), cats were considered to be evil or bad omens, while in others they were revered as deities (in ancient Egypt), or associated with gods (Scandinavian and Hindu lore). In dreams, cats express the feminine, or anima, as they are independent, soft, affectionate, clever, and unpredictable. They can also stand for the mysterious and magical (as a result of their legendary association with witches).

Dog

Dogs are a near-universal symbol of fidelity. In Africa and other countries, dogs are considered to be the wise creatures from which civilization descended. Early Christians linked sheepdogs, who watch over and guard their flocks, with priests. In their protective aspect, dogs are admired in Japan, especially for their help to women and children. In medieval times, white dogs were often depicted at the feet of various religious figures as symbols of piety.

But dogs have a darker symbolism, as well. In ancient Egypt and Greece, dog-like beings guarded the underworld, and were thus associated with death. For Muslims, the dog is the companion of the devil. Dogs can also represent the negative, aggressive animus, especially when they attack.

Horse

Horses are associated with energy ("horsepower"), either in harmony or in conflict. Horses frequently symbolize war, and can represent death (death rides a horse in various myths; death accompanies the Four Horsemen of the Apocalypse; even the fearsome death-bringing wraiths in Tolkien's *Lord of the Rings* trilogy ride dark horses). In other myths, horses represent the archetype of the mother. Jung described the horse as symbolizing intuition and baser

instincts, whereas Freudians associate the horse with sexuality.

Rabbit, hare

Rabbits symbolize unrestrained sexuality and procreation. Different cultures, depending upon their values, have given either positive or negative connotations to these qualities of the rabbit. Rabbits also represent quickness. In China, the hare symbolizes feminine energy, as it does in many other countries, as well as long life. The rabbit or hare is also a manifestation of the trickster archetype, for example Brer Rabbit and the White Rabbit in Alice in Wonderland. Tricksters are seen to cross freely between the unconscious and conscious minds, playing tricks on consciousness.

Mythical Animals

Animals of legend and mythology are associated with magic. In fairy tales and other lore, they represent the magical and mysterious power of uniqueness (and, often, of deformity). They also signal transformation. In dreams, these figures are very rarely seen, but are sometimes mentioned as emblems, or as characters in books.

Dragons

Dragons were symbols of evil in chivalry tales during the Middle Ages. Dragons, who guard their treasure (gold, a virgin, or eggs), and fight all intruders, may be symbols of the mother. In early dragon stories, the dragons that were slayed were females who were protecting their brood. The dragon, who must be met, faced, and conquered, is an element in the hero's journey and we all face dragons throughout our lives and development. In the hero's journey myth, the dragon to be vanquished is our relationship to our mother, the contents of our childhood unconscious. One must psychologically separate from the mother and survive the separation in order to become an adult.

Monsters

Animalistic monsters are the ultimate shadow projections, that is, they represent what is most threatening and unknown within us.

Unicorns

Legend holds that only a virgin can capture a unicorn. In fairy stories, unicorns symbolize purity. In China, they represent kindness and gentleness.

The following categories may also have resonance:

Cats
PAGE 232

Vocations (mystical occupations)
PAGE 221

Cold-blooded Creatures

Almost everyone has had dreams about snakes, crocodiles or alligators, which were some of the first animals on Earth. Cold-blooded, these animals need external sources to provide them with warmth to enable them to survive. Dreams about them are often archetypal, and their symbolism is complex. Dreaming of cold-blooded animals suggests one's mood and general well-being may be too dependent on others or on outside circumstances. These animals also have scaly skin, which suggests protectiveness.

Snakes

The snake is a paradoxical symbol across cultures. Jung wrote that the snake in a dream could mean many things: the past, future, a feminine unconscious force, or illness. By some, it is believed to denote pure evil, while others see it as representing healing and wisdom. Today, the caduceus symbol (two snakes entwined on a staff) symbolizes medicine. The snake is also seen as a symbol of death and rebirth (it sheds its skin); sexual, kundalini energy in the East (Gnostics also related the snake to the spinal cord); and for psychoanalysts, the libido and phallus (its shape and movement).

Threatening snake

Dreaming of a threatening snake (one that is actually threatening you, rather than just the feeling that it could, if it chose, hurt you) implies that you are afraid of the meaning the snake is holding for you. Consider why you would be dreaming about this now. Is something happening in your waking world to evoke this fear?

Being bitten by a snake

Snakes inject venom into their victims by opening their mouths and biting. Sometimes, dreams of being bitten by a snake can represent the hurtful power of words. Being bitten also suggests that the dreamer is being, or in danger of being, poisoned by something in the unconscious.

Observing a snake

Any time you are observing an object or character in a dream, your ego is working hard. Observing a snake might mean that you are taking a cool, objective look at these unconscious parts of yourself, determining how dangerous they might be, and whether or not it is safe to approach them . . . but cautiously.

A snake biting its tail

This image is called the *ouroboros* among Gnostics and alchemists, who see it as a symbol of time and eternity, and of nature continually returning to its origin.

Lizards

These animals are interpreted similarly to snakes.

>

The following category may also have resonance:

Q&A ego

PAGE 144

Crocodiles and alligators

Along with turtles, these animals have remained unchanged since the time of the dinosaurs. They are ancient creatures, and as such, can symbolize in dreams very old patterns of behavior and feeling—all that is "ancient" within us. (Sometimes dreams of dinosaurs also accomplish this purpose.) Alligators and crocodiles represent universal experiences of birth and death. In medieval times, these animals were thought to be related to the dragon, and were believed to guard treasure and wisdom. Finally, the phrase "crocodile tears," suggesting false emotion, may be important for you if a crocodile appears in your dreams.

Being among them

If you dream you are among crocodiles or alligators, in a swamp, perhaps, or observing them at a zoo or from safe, dry land, you are dreaming about something ancient and possibly collective. Consider if something troublesome from your own far-distant past might be surfacing now.

Being threatened

Crocodile and alligator dreams are most often frightening, so that aspect of these dreams should not be over-interpreted. These animals are rarely depicted as friendly or nurturing—what we are the least familiar with tends to frighten us the most.

The following categories may
also have resonance:

$\mathcal{W}$ater
PAGE 198

$Q\&A$ mythical
animals
PAGE 234

Birds

The only type of animal to cross nearly all cultures in dreams is the bird, which universally symbolizes soaring thought, imagination, and the soul after death. In the Koran, birds represent one's fate. High-flying birds suggest spiritual longing, while dreaming of a caged bird suggests your spirit is being confined. A dream of a sick or dying bird may symbolize a deep transformation at the level of the soul.

Dove

These birds were associated with female deities in the ancient world. Islam holds the dove as sacred, and it symbolizes the Holy Spirit in Christianity.

A dove holding an olive branch

This is a symbol of peace, which originated in the Bible.

Two white doves

Two white doves represent the archetype of love and relationship; modern weddings often feature the release of doves for this reason.

Eagle

The eagle was the companion of the highest gods and heroes of several ancient societies. It symbolizes rebirth and clear sight. But on the negative side, it can also suggest too much pride and desire for power. The eagle is the symbol of Saint John, and of many powerful nations.

Eagle in flight

Eagles soaring free can represent the feeling of liberty we have after a great achievement in our career or personal life. They may also suggest far-sightedness and clear vision, a larger perspective than could be gained on the ground.

Endangered eagle

Dreaming of an eagle in danger (which they are, in reality) may serve as a warning that your ability to see clearly is in danger or compromised, or, alternatively, that an injury to your pride has occurred.

The following categories may also have resonance:

Mountains and Hills
PAGE 190

The heavens
PAGE 188

Q&A flying
PAGE 38

Owl

The owl's meaning is contradictory: for most peoples, it stands for wisdom, and also for evil. In Egyptian hieroglyphs, the owl stands for death and night.

Unseen owl calling at night

Hearing distinctive sounds other than people talking is relatively rare in dreams. If you do dream of an owl calling at night, though, consider what you might be trying to tell yourself. Then listen.

Underwater

As discussed in Part One, water is one element that all dream experts agree represents life and the unconscious (particularly feeling). Psychologically, then, animals that live in the sea represent messengers who communicate between the unconscious and conscious minds. They also have spiritual or religious connotations, living, as they do, in an element so different from our own.

Fishes

In Buddhism, the golden fish is the symbol of enlightenment. Fish symbolized the secrecy of early Christians, and also the rite of baptism.

School of fish

In China, a school of fish represents wealth and fertility.

Shark

As fearsome creatures of the deep whose eyes have a glazed, deadened look, sharks in dreams may represent death, or the fear of being devoured or "ripped apart" by one's unconscious feelings and impulses. In the U.S. we speak of dishonest, greedy people as sharks.

Sea mammals

Here, dreams provide the intersection between the symbology of the ocean, mammals, and our own sense of ourselves as humans. We ascribe to dolphins and whales quite lofty human qualities.

Dolphin

The dolphin plays a role in the mythology of most cultures that live near the ocean. Dolphins were considered sacred in Greece, and were associated with several gods and goddesses. In legends where friendly dolphins help humans, dolphins represent salvation arising unexpectedly from the depths.

Whale

The symbolism of whales is among the most impressive of all animals. They abound in myths and legends, where they are treated as wise, spiritual creatures who live at the boundary between heaven and earth. Whales may also symbolize creativity. In some cultures and art, however, whales are depicted as evil, or as representing and evoking the duality of ultimate good and evil (*Moby Dick*).

Most importantly, whales are one of the only symbols we have of the entire world.

The following category may also have resonance:

*W*ater (ocean)
PAGE 200

Buildings and Other Structures

WHERE YOUR DREAM TAKES place provides a context for the action that occurs. But more than being just a backdrop, your dream's setting can provide clues as to the meaning of the dream as a whole. Many people's dream settings comprise a dream theme that recurs throughout their lives, and this is especially true when it comes to buildings. As discussed on pages 102 and 248, childhood homes are one such common dream theme.

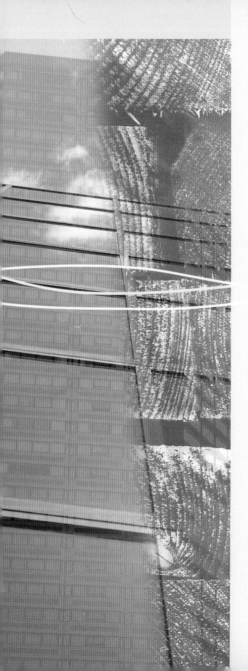

Whether your dream takes place in your own home, that of someone else, a work building, or some other structure, note the quality of the dream building. What is it made of? In what condition is it? If it is a familiar building, does it look the same way as it does in real life? Do you feel safe in this building? Do you feel at home in it? Answering these initial questions will help you to unlock the building's meaning as you read through the rest of this chapter.

Houses

Along with water, houses are an agreed-upon symbol among psychologists. In dreams, houses represent layers of the psyche. Looked at this way, house dreams can be fascinating. From now on, when someone tells you a dream about exploring a house, you can translate the dream for yourself as a map of the dreamer's conscious and unconscious mind. What is in there? Is it unfamiliar or dark? (The dreamer is dreaming about unconscious feelings and thoughts.) Or is it familiar and sun-filled? (This house contains mostly what the dreamer already knows about herself.) Is it old? (Not much change has happened there.) Or is it new? (Transformations are afoot.)

General characteristics

Your dream may or may not include the following house elements. No matter what kind of house you are dreaming of—your own, or someone else's—these descriptions may apply.

Kitchen

Of all the rooms in a dream house, the kitchen most represents feminine nurturance— that is, the mother. For better or worse, most of us grew up in kitchens where our mothers cooked for us. What happens in your dream kitchen, and even its condition, can relate to your feelings about your mother, your own motherhood, or nurturance and care-giving in general. What "feeds" you? And how well? Because the kitchen is the place where substances are transformed, it is also similar to the wizard's or witch's cave in fairy tales, where potions are brewed and change is instigated.

Bedroom

Some dream experts believe that whatever happens in a dream bedroom is actually about the dreamer's sexuality. This setting may also relate to intimacy more generally, as the bedroom is where we may be most completely private and ourselves.

Bathroom

Bathroom dreams seem to appear most often when people are dealing with their emotional baggage. You have to go to the bathroom and can't find one, or it is filthy, or the door isn't there or won't close or lock, or there is something wrong with the toilet, or you overflow it! In each case, ask yourself how you are feeling about other people seeing the less desirable parts of yourself, and how you are feeling about those parts. Exposed? Dirty? Bad? As if you have too much? (Of course, people also have these dreams when they just have to use the bathroom at night.)

Living room

The living room is where you spend most of your time, and as such, what happens there may simply represent your life—the way you conduct yourself day-to-day, and what is most important to you.

Basement

The basement is the bottom, deepest level of the house, and therefore corresponds to the unconscious and what lies within that part of the mind.

Attic

Attics, as the highest level, represent clear consciousness. "Attic" is used linguistically in English as a metaphor for memory (i.e., "clearing the cobwebs out of the attic"), and of the mind, in general.

Foundation

What is your psyche built upon? Is the foundation firm or shaky? Are you redoing what supports the rest of you? Is your house built on solid ground, straight onto the earth, or are you upon shaky stilts?

Stairway

Stairways are classical Freudian symbols for sexual intercourse. Other schools of dream interpretation see stairs in a different light, as connections between different levels of the psyche. If you dream of a blocked stairway, that might suggest you are having difficulty becoming fully aware of something within you, or have not yet made the connection.

Outside versus inside

Being outside a house looking in implies that you are gaining an objective view of yourself—from a distance. The outside of a house symbolizes the way you present yourself to the world. Being inside, then, suggests that you are being introspective about yourself and your current situation. However, real-life experiences influence whether you dream of being indoors or outdoors. If you spend appreciably more time in or out, then you are more likely to dream of yourself that way. There is also a sex difference: women dream of being inside houses more frequently than do men, who are most often outdoors in their dreams.

People within

People within houses can be viewed as representing themselves, as you know them in the real world, but also as parts of your own psyche (see Chapter 3).

Childhood house

Although you haven't lived there for many years, you may dream of your childhood house. Perhaps it is blended with your own home, or a friend's house, or even a workplace building. Such a dream shows you that your unconscious is unclear whether or not what's happening now is really happening now, with the people you presently know, or whether you are, in fact, back in your own past, with the people you knew then. Dreams like this help alert you to the ways in which you might be misunderstanding a current situation—reading into it the qualities and characteristics of people long gone. Alternatively, they may help you to consider what the similarities really are between now and then (see also page 102). Dreaming of your childhood house with you being the age you were then can give you a vivid sense of exactly what life was like for you in the past, or it may portray childlike feelings in a current situation.

Your own home

Perhaps the most important of all of our house dreams are those in which our own home appears. In these dreams, we produce a sort of "dream film" depicting the inside of our own minds. Being inside your own home is the most common indoor dream setting. But your home can appear in a number of ways, each of them meaningful.

Just as it is

Dreaming of your house exactly as it is does happen. If there is nothing strange about your dream house, and nothing unusual is happening within it, you might take this dream as a simple, straightforward

representation of your waking life concerns.

Distorted

Often your dream house will be different from your real-life house in some way. It might have elements of a past house or completely different setting, it may change as the dream progresses, or it may be called your house in the dream even though you don't recognize it. All of these images can be meaningful. Because dreams of houses seem to represent the psyche, when our dream house is different from our real house, that signals a change—sometimes a major one—is occurring within us. We may be learning something new about ourselves, realizing we carry parts of the past with us, or discovering more about who we are.

>

Discovering new rooms

You are in your real-life house, turn a corner, and suddenly there is a whole new room. I have seen numerous clients who have had this dream during their psychotherapy. Because we don't know how many people have this dream who are not in therapy, we can't say that it is related to doing intensive work within oneself. But these dreams do seem to occur when dreamers are discovering new things about themselves. Often the new rooms are discovered with delight. Sometimes, they are frightening and unsettling, as dreamers face the unknown. If you have such a dream and get inside the new room, recall carefully what inhabited it. What was the furniture like? Was anyone inside? What kind of person would live in such a room? In short, what does the physical appearance of the room suggest about a recently discovered part of you?

Remodeling or destroying

These dreams are also common among psychotherapy clients, although I notice they tend to occur during dramatic times of change or crisis. Sometimes you can alter parts of yourself, your attitudes or beliefs, by doing a little remodeling job within the psyche. Other times, when you are transforming how you respond to and understand others, view yourself, or perceive the world, the change requires demolition of the old "house." Out with the old, and in with the new! If the change was sparked by an external crisis, you may dream of your house being destroyed, often by fire, or (especially in California) by an earthquake. The former suggests purification (see page 196); the latter, a dramatic "shift in one's ground."

House of friends or family

Dreaming of being in the home of a friend or family member occurs less frequently than being in your own home. Nevertheless, these dreams can be informative.

Just as it is

Again, if your dream takes place in another's home, and it looks just like it does in waking life, consider this dream to be about the action and interactions within the house, rather than about the house's potential symbolism.

Distorted

Houses of friends or family that appear differently to the way they are in real life can be explored in the same way as dreams of your own house. A distorted house implies something about your connection with the person whose house this is. They may be helping you to find new aspects of yourself, or introducing new interests or perspectives to you.

Alternatively, you may be seeing something in the house's owner that you have not seen before.

Their house is your house
You dream that you are at a friend's house, yet you know it is actually your house. Perhaps you are letting into yourself some quality of your friend, or discovering that quality within your own psyche. Alternatively, you may dream of a house you've never seen before, but in the dream, it is yours. In real life, perhaps you are being asked to perform or behave in a way so unfamiliar to you, in a work situation or relationship, that your own house feels unknown. Take note of the quality and style of the house for clues to the persona required of you (see page 14).

Often when the dream house is your house, you seem to believe, in the dream, that you really live there and have no sense of your real-life house.

Such a dream can be a metaphor for feeling at home in an unfamiliar, new place—either within yourself or in the external world.

Famous houses
Dreaming of a famous house is similar to dreaming of a famous person (see page 212). The difference, here, is that you are dreaming of the setting that surrounds the famous person, and their lifestyle, rather than their personality. A lifestyle can be adopted by anyone with the means, just as a social role can (see page 14). Famous house dreams are often persona dreams. Which social role are you exploring, desiring, or criticizing?

You live there
When you have the unusual dream of actually living in a famous person's house, it suggests that you are identified with the

persona that person represents. It may also signal to you that you have gone too far and have lost your sense of the rest of your personality. You may be living your life as if you had only the qualities of the persona, and your real self could be languishing.

Being invited there by the famous person
These dreams are more common than actually living in the house yourself. You dream you have been summoned to Buckingham Palace by the Queen; you are the special guest of the Osbournes; Elvis awaits you at Graceland … Think about who this famous person is; what are their outstanding qualities and what are they famous for? Are these aspects of yourself, as well? Can you develop these qualities in a playful way? Or, alternatively, could you be overdoing it? Is the rest of yourself getting time to play?

Workplace

Dreams of buildings associated with work suggest that you are working on something—both inside and outside. Outside, of course, you most likely have a real job in a real building, even if that setting is a home office. If you dream of that real-life setting, the building itself may be just a backdrop. In such a case, the people and their interactions will be more important than the architecture.

However, do consider the questions raised in the introduction to this chapter. They can help you reveal dream metaphors for feelings you may be having about your real-life job.

Workplace that is not your own

Dreaming of a workplace that is not your own might just reflect the inner, often unconscious, work you are doing on your own psyche: adapting, coping, changing, forming new perceptions, questioning old beliefs, discovering new things about yourself and others. What kind of work are you doing inside? Pay attention to the building's age, for it can be a clue as to how long you have been working on this particular inner challenge.

Factories

Dreams of factories suggest production: something is being made that, we hope, will be useful. If you dream of a factory and do not work in one, your dream might take place in a dark, dingy, labor-intensive factory. Stereotypical, almost Dickensian environments, tend to appear in the dreams of those unacquainted with the modern factory setting. Some of my clients dream of factories when they feel dehumanized by their work, as if they were just a cog in a wheel, or a number in a large machine.

Working in a factory

What is your career situation? Are you slaving away at something? Do you feel overwhelmed with tasks? Or are you whistling while you work? Answering these questions might help you to clarify your true feelings about your job. If your responses feel negative, is there a way to change your physical work environment to brighten it or to introduce some humanity there?

Children in a factory

The true Dickens dream! I have only heard this dream once, so it is extremely rare. Still, if you happen to dream of children working in a factory, you might wonder whether or not you are having enough fun in your life. Are you enslaving the young, enthusiastic, playful parts of you?

Inside your own workplace
Just as it is

As with houses, if you dream of your work as it is in the waking world, the interactions you have within will be more important than the setting will.

Different workplaces blended

Are you having a difficult time at work, or with a co-worker or boss? Is this situation reminding you of something you experienced in the other setting? Try to realistically appraise the similarities and differences (ask a friend for help, if you need to), and brainstorm new ways of coping with the current situation. Perhaps something you did then can help now?

People who don't belong

If you dream of family or friends being at work when they don't work where you do in real life, this may be a sign that your work has invaded other aspects of your life. Also, your experiences with these other people may be coloring your perceptions of your current work situation. Finally, these dream characters might be helpful in solving work problems: in waking life, what would these people do in your situation?

Solving a problem

Any time you solve a problem in a dream, it is worth taking time to consider whether or not what you did in the dream might work in the waking world. As we saw in Part One, some people do use dreams to solve problems and for inspiration (see page 54).

Skyscrapers

For decades to come, the image of the terrorist attack on New York will probably accompany thoughts of skyscrapers for many of us. Those images have made their way into the dreams of people all over the world. Even before that tragedy occurred, skyscrapers appeared in dreams as symbols of high aspirations regarding one's profession or career path. It may be that now the meaning will change for many of us to symbolize feelings of exposure, horror, and a shocking vulnerability.

Mirrored exterior

As a metaphor for oneself, a mirrored skyscraper suggests a permanently sunglasses-wearing persona: you can see out, but others can't see inside of you. In some professions, this is an asset. In one's personal life, however, it can be at most a disastrous, and at least, a lonely way of life.

Taking an elevator

Are you being assisted in your journey? Is it smooth and comfortable? Are there many stops along the way? Are others traveling with you? Do you know where you are going, or are you relying on others to direct you?

Going up or down

Are you going up (sense of success, but may also be an inflated, "too high" view of yourself)? Or are you going down (sense of failure, or gaining a more grounded, realistic view of your capabilities)? If the elevator is broken, check your motivation and any inner blocks you may be experiencing regarding your career. Then use the elevator phone to call for repair.

Can't find the door

Are you in a skyscraper and lost? Is there no door? Such a motif suggests you may have become "lost" in your work persona. If so, take a little time to relax and enjoy other aspects of your life.

Society

Buildings apart from our own homes, may represent a variety of aspects of ourselves and the society in which we live. Jung saw cities as symbolizing the mother, and the feminine in general; cities provide shelter for those who live there. In the Bible, and in English and many other languages, cities are described as feminine.

Schools

Schools are places where we go to learn new things and to develop as people. Dreams of being in school, then, suggest you are educating yourself in some sense, or need to do so.

Grade level

Is the lesson you are learning elementary (primary school) or complex (university level)? Grade level in dreams can stand for the difficulty of the problem you are grappling with.

Being in school

Besides the theme of being back in school and learning you haven't yet graduated (see page 20), another quite common dream theme is being unprepared for an exam. You haven't studied, the exam begins, and you don't know how you are going to perform. These dreams often occur when you are feeling tested by an unfamiliar situation, or are applying a new skill. As psychologist Alfred Adler wrote, the individual meaning of a test-taking dream could be to remind you that you have passed tests before, and you will pass this one, too. It could also suggest that you are not prepared to face the task before you. Make sure you consider the dream as a whole—its feeling, tone, and the way in which it ends—before determining which meaning (if either) applies to your test-taking dream.

Religious buildings

Some schools of thought hold that contained, religious buildings represent the soul or self, in the same way that houses symbolize the individual's psyche. Dreams of being within a religious building may speak to your spiritual condition, longings, or needs.

Churches and temples

As physical representatives of organized religion, churches and temples are places where rites are held, including those relating to momentous events in the life cycle. As such, they may speak to eternal themes of birth, aging, and death as they appear in your own life. These structures are also hallowed places. Consider what being in such a location means to you, and what you feel when you are there.   >

Monasteries

Monasteries are more mysterious to most of us than churches or temples are. They are also associated with the masculine, asceticism, and devotion. In a monastery, one is completely focused on one's spiritual life.

Natural sacred sites

You might dream of being in an ancient, natural locale that is considered sacred. These dreams might be archetypal (see Chapter 1), containing themes of a universal nature. Often, natural sacred sites are related to the underworld, death, and rebirth. Investigating the history of your dream site might help you to further explore its collective meaning. (See also landscapes, page 190.)

Stores

When you dream of a store, especially if you are inside one, consider what you are shopping for, as this may relate to something you seek or need in the waking world or within yourself. Also notice who you are shopping with. If you are alone, this may be something you need to find on your own. If you are with a trusted ally, perhaps she or he can help you locate it.

Clothing store

Clothing is a prime symbol of the persona (see page 14), the social mask we wear in society. What kind of clothes do you seek? If you're an artist and you dream that you're shopping for a suit, perhaps you need to develop your business acumen. Shopping for clothes, in general, suggests you are looking for new roles to try. Notice which clothes you choose, and especially whether or not you buy any.

Sports store

Shopping in a sports-oriented store suggests you are seeking new ways to express your physicality, or to update old exercise or recreation routines into the present. Sports are quite metaphorical. For instance, snow skiing may symbolize skimming along the surface of frozen feeling; water skiing, boating, and surfing, along the surface of the unconscious. Hiking is a wonderful metaphor for the hero's journey, and the game of golf has recently been portrayed in books and movies as an allegory for spiritual development.

Gift store

Are you searching for something to give someone else? What gift do you want or need to provide? Is it an object that needs to be given, or what does the object represent? In what ways are you already giving?

Garden store

Garden stores relate to the symbolism of the garden more generally (see page 192). If you are looking for plants or objects to enhance your garden, that suggests you are nurturing your more feminine qualities. What does your garden need?   >

Financial institutions

Financial buildings are, of course, related to the meaning of money. As places where money is primary, dreams of financial institutions can give you information regarding your approach to and feelings about money, as well as the way in which you manage it. How large the building is may reflect how large the issue looms in your mind, how much energy it consumes. The condition of the building may give you a clue as to how secure you feel financially, and, since money is a metaphor itself, how safe you feel in the world in general. In the Western world, money can also represent your life energy. In reality, of course, money is just an impersonal means of exchange, with no relationship to your ultimate value as a person.

Banks

Where are you investing your energy? Is it safe? How much do you have stored up? Is this an old bank (suggesting old, perhaps outdated, attitudes about money)? Is it modern, but impersonal (implying you may need to rethink where you are investing yourself)?

Offices of financial advisers

These are the places we go to seek help and advice, so considering the competence and physical surroundings of advisers in dreams is always a good idea. Is your dream money adviser up to the task? Is he or she straightforward and clear? The identity of your financial advisers and the way in which they handle money can give you information about the way you are handling your own need for security.

Government offices

Dreams of government and other political themes are rare. Even during times of war and other forms of societal tumult, researchers found that most of our dreams are about our own personal, daily concerns. It is extremely unusual to dream of societal problems.

As you've already seen, viewing parts of your dream as pictures of corresponding parts of yourself can aid you in understanding the meaning of your nightly visions. Government offices perform functions similar to those of the ego (see page 145). They administer, analyse, mediate between opposing needs, and provide essential functions for society. As reflected by governmental agencies that may appear in your dreams, how well is your ego doing its job? How strong and sturdy is the structure (building) that contains these functions?

Political offices

These are where the administrative, objective functions of the psyche reside. How well are you governing yourself? Do you like and admire those who hold power over you? Or do they need some retraining or a values adjustment?

Social service offices

Welfare, health, employment, mental health, and other social service offices relate to the caregiving, feeling aspects of the psyche, as well as to self-nurturance. Are yours adequate and helpful, or crumbling and losing funding (being deprived of internal energy)?

Legal offices

Legal agencies are the dominion of the superego (see pages 144–145)—our conscience—which tries to make us behave in accordance with what we believe to be right and may punish us when we do something that feels wrong. Ideally, one's conscience and pleasure-seeking drives are held in balance by the ego, which tries to get us as much of what we want as is possible, without losing the love and respect of others and society. How is your psyche at maintaining this balance?

Entertainment venues

Dreams of places where we pursue pleasure can inform us about how often and how freely we allow ourselves to have fun, or, in the language of some pop psychologists, allow our "inner child" to play. Consider your dream settings. How many of them are play (versus work) locations? If you have only a few entertainment venues in your dreams, perhaps it's time to let yourself run loose.

Restaurants and bars

Places where we nourish ourselves and socialize, such as restaurants and cafés, can be nurturing places. Someone asks what you want, makes an effort to produce it for you, then cleans up after you when you've finished. Restaurants, for some dream experts, are like kitchens: feminine places of maternal nourishment. We seek them out in life when we are in need of maternal energy. We may dream of them when mothering, nourishment, or nurturing are an issue in our lives. Or they may simply reflect your own tendency to eat out a lot. If you dream of going to a bar, or of getting drunk, when this is not something you typically or regularly do, consider whether or not you are ignoring something important in your life. Some people dream of being drunk as a metaphor for willful unconsciousness and being unable or unwilling to discriminate or make difficult decisions in the outside world.

Theatres

In theatres, we watch others performing roles for us. As discussed in Part One, what happens inside a dream theatre can be very meaningful. Look at the building—is the play, film, or concert taking place in a real theatre, or is the theatre another familiar building such as your workplace or home? If this is the case, you might consider in what way your work or home life may feel unreal to you. Are you overdramatizing? Playing a part? Next, try to assess how old the theatre is, as often the age of buildings in dreams can point to how long you have been playing a particular role or dealing with a certain issue.

Sports stadiums

Sports events involve strong, physical competition. Dreaming of a sports stadium, even if no sporting event is taking place there, may indicate your feelings about your own physical condition, age, or ability to compete.

Amusement/Theme parks

If you dream of an amusement park, your psyche is setting the scene in a place where crowds of people go to have fun. Theme parks are mostly populated by younger people and older people with children. They are playgrounds for adrenaline, evoking childlike, thrilling feelings of fear and conquest.

When you dream of such a place, you may be getting a view of your child ego state, being reminded of what it felt like to be a child, and reconsidering the place of fun in your life. While at college I was surprised at how many of my fellow students had amusement park dreams, and these dreams seemed to be expressing the longing for carefree fun in the midst of constant, real-life, adult ego challenges.

Roller coasters

These can be among the most humorous of all dreams, once you understand their metaphorical meaning. Most of us have used the phrase "it was like a roller coaster" to describe an unsettling, inconsistent situation or relationship. Life, itself, with all its changes, unexpected twists, turns, hills, drops, fears, and exhilaration, can also be like a roller coaster. No wonder, then, that roller coasters tend to appear in your dreams when you are experiencing change.

Bibliography

Dement, W., *Some Must Watch While Some Must Sleep* (1972, San Francisco: W.H. Freeman [Sleep, REM studies, and dreaming]

Domhoff, G. W., *Finding Meaning in Dreams: A Quantitative Approach* (1996, New York: Plenum) [What people dream about; how to do your own research on dreams; comprehensive review of dream content studies]

Foulkes, D., *Children's Dreams: Longitudinal Studies* (1982, New York: Wiley) [Results of studies on children's dreams]

Fowles, J., *The Magus* (1978, New York: Bantam) [An exquisite, dream-like novel]

Freud, S., *The Interpretation of Dreams* (1953, New York: Basic Books) [Freud's original ideas on symbol interpretation and the dreamwork processes]

Freud, S., *On Dreams* (1952, New York: Norton). [A summary of his ideas on dreams] Gackenbach, J., & Bosveld, J., Control Your Dreams (1989, New York: Harper & Row). [Dream control experts]

Hall, C., & Van de Castle, R. L., *The Content Analysis of Dreams* (1966, New York: Appleton-Century-Crofts) [Classic book of dream norms–what people dream about]

Hartmann, E., *Boundaries of the Mind* (1992, New York: Basic Books) [Nightmare expert on how "thin boundaries" may produce more nightmares]

Hartmann, E., *Dreams and Nightmares* (1998, New York: Plenum) [Information on nightmares and dreaming in general]

Hilton, J., *Lost Horizon* (1990, Pleasantville NY: Reader's Digest) [Mysterious and beautiful novel; quoted on page 136]

Johnson, R., *Inner Work* (1986, New York: Harper & Row) [For learning how to use active imagination with your dream characters]

Jung, C. G., *The Archetypes and the Collective Unconscious* [Explains archetypes, including the shadow, persona, anima/animus, and how to meet them through dream interpretation]

Jung, C. G., *Man and His Symbols* (1964, Garden City, NJ: Doubleday) [Written just before his death, a chapter on dream interpretation]

Jung, C. G., *Memories, Dreams, Reflections* (1965, New York: Vantage) [His autobiography, including his journey into dream work]

Jung, C. G., *Dreams* (1974, Trans. R.F.C. Hull. Princeton, NJ: Princeton Univ. Press) [Collection of his ideas on dreams]

Jung, E., *Animus and Anima* (1957, Dallas: Spring Pubs) [Classic work on these archetypes and how they appear in dreams]

LaBerge, S., *Lucid Dreaming* (1986, New York: Ballantine) [Lucid dreaming expert shows you how]

Lakoff, G., *Women, Fire, and Dangerous Things* (1987, Chicago: University of Chicago Press) [Linguist discusses metaphor in language]

Maybruck, P., *Pregnancy and Dreams* (1989, Los Angeles: Tarcher) [Research on how dreams change with pregnancy]

Nathan, S., "Cross-cultural perspectives on penis envy" (1981, *Psychiatry*, 44, 39-44) [This study suggested phallic symbols represent power, not the penis!]

Shafton, A., *Dream Reader: Contemporary Approaches to the Understanding of Dreams* (1995, New York: SUNY Press) [Fascinating, fact-filled book on the findings of dream reasearch all over the world]

Tonay, V.K., *The Creative Dreamer's Journal and Workbook* (1997, Berkeley: Celestial Arts) [A place to record your most personal dreams; sleep and dreaming tips]

Tonay, V.K., To hear the NPR interview referred to on page 20, go to www.npr.org and search the archives under dreams and 7/10/99.

Ullman, M., Krippner, S., & Vaughan, A., *Dream Telepathy* (1973, New York: Macmillan) [Research findings on telepathic dreams]

Van de Castle, R. L., *Our Dreaming Mind* (1994, New York: Random House) [Comprehensive dream research findings on all topics, and interesting commentary]

Van de Castle, R. L., "Animal figures in fantasy and dreams." In A. Katcher and A. Beck (Eds.), *New Perspectives on our Lives with Companion Animals* (1983, Philadelphia: Univ. of Pennsylvania Press)

von Franz, M.-L., Puer Aeturnus (1970, Sigo Press) [Jungian analyst illuminates the archetype of the eternal child]

Wilmer, H., "Vietnam and madness: Dreams of schizophrenic veterans" (1982, *Journal of the American Academy of Psychoanalysis*, 10, 47–65)

Index

Acknowledgments

I am grateful to the editorial team at Collins & Brown. I quickly realized that, thanks to them, this book would be published with integrity and style. The beauty of the book stuns me. Caroline Grimshaw is a very creative artist; I feel fortunate to have been graced with her work. Thanks also to the marketing and sales staff who will be responsible for getting this volume into your hands.

One never writes a book alone, or from only one's own personal experience. Always, we are touched by others and changed by them as we go through life. My dream group and psychotherapy clients over the years have taught me much about the many meanings of dreams, and sleep.

Each of them has contributed to what I know, and I am thankful for their courage. Students and colleagues in the world of dream work have been helpful, too. I would like to particularly acknowledge my late friend and mentor, psychology researcher Dr. Frank "Xave" Barron, who encouraged me to study, work with, and make real all kinds of dreams.

Please visit my website, www.drtonay.com, for more information on dreams and tips for exploring your dream world. I enjoy getting mail! If you'd like to be on my mailing list, please feel free to email:

www.VeronicaTonay.com

or write to:

Veronica Tonay, PhD

P. O. Box 568

Santa Cruz, CA 95061, USA

Thank you for buying this book, and sweet dreams!

pages 66–67, 70 © Tom Stewart/CORBIS; page 80 © Galen Rowell/CORBIS; page 80 © Jim Zuckerman/CORBIS; pages 112–113, 166–167 © Mark J. Tweedie; Ecoscene/CORBIS; pages 144, 145 © Barry Lewis/CORBIS; page 144 The Art Archive/Ashmolean Museum Oxford/Eileen Tweedy; page 150 © Myron Jay Dorf/CORBIS; page 150 © George B. Diebold/CORBIS; pages 174–175, 176 © Henry Blackham/CORBIS; pages 204-205 © Ondrea Barbe/CORBIS; pages 212-213 © Jon Roca/Rex Features; page 214 © Action Press/Rex Features; page 215 © Neils Jorgensen/Rex Features; pages 218–219 © Rob Lewine/CORBIS; pages 222-223 Barbara Bellingham/Getty Images; pages 232–233 © Jim Zuckerman/CORBIS; pages 234-235 © The Art Archive/Dagli Orti; pages 250-251 Theo Aloffs/Getty Images; pages 258–259 © LWA-Dann Tardif/CORBIS; pages 260–261 © Alan Schein Photography/CORBIS